ROMANESQUE ARCHITECTURE
IN
WESTERN EUROPE

BY

A. W. CLAPHAM
C.B.E., F.B.A., F.S.A.

OXFORD
AT THE CLARENDON PRESS
1936

In collaboration with the
COURTAULD INSTITUTE OF ART
UNIVERSITY OF LONDON

BYZANTINE ART
By D. TALBOT RICE. 1935

ROMANESQUE ARCHITECTURE
IN WESTERN EUROPE
By A. W. CLAPHAM. 1936

PRINTED IN GREAT BRITAIN
AT THE UNIVERSITY PRESS, OXFORD
BY JOHN JOHNSON, PRINTER TO THE UNIVERSITY

ROMANESQUE ARCHITECTURE
IN
WESTERN EUROPE

OXFORD
UNIVERSITY PRESS
AMEN HOUSE, E.C. 4
LONDON EDINBURGH GLASGOW NEW YORK
TORONTO MELBOURNE CAPETOWN BOMBAY
CALCUTTA MADRAS SHANGHAI
HUMPHREY MILFORD
PUBLISHER TO THE
UNIVERSITY

SANTIAGO CATHEDRAL. SPAIN. 1078–*c*. 1145
Interior of Nave

PREFACE

THE chapters comprising this book are an amplification of a series of lectures first delivered to the Courtauld Institute of Art in 1932 and in a slightly different form for the Faculty of Modern History at Oxford in the same year. The intention has been to present a general survey of the architecture and architectural sculpture of each country during the period under review, with the idea of determining the local forms of Romanesque expression, rather than providing an account of individual buildings. When a building or work has been the subject of controversy I have attempted to give some idea of the contending points of view and of my own conclusions on the matter in question. Footnotes and references have been reduced to a minimum, the principal modern works on each branch of the subject being cited in a bibliography at the end of each chapter. The subject has not been pursued beyond the beginnings of the Gothic style, and the book does not profess to give an account of the transition between the two periods.

I have to acknowledge the assistance of my friends, Mr. E. A. Ralegh Radford and Dr. W. M. Whitehill, in reading the Italian and Spanish sections of the book respectively and for many emendations and suggestions. I am also indebted to Miss V. M. Dallas for compiling the index.

I have in addition to acknowledge the kindness of Mr. G. E. Chambers, Mr. Arthur Gardner, Mr. J. R. H. Weaver, Dr. W. M. Whitehill, and Mr. F. T. A. Power in permitting me to use their photographs. To many others, whose names are indicated in the List of Illustrations, I am also indebted.

A. W. C.

LONDON, 1935.

CONTENTS

LIST OF ILLUSTRATIONS

Santiago Cathedral, Spain. 1078–*c*. 1145. Interior of Nave.
Photograph by Ruiz Vernacci, Madrid.   *Frontispiece.*

PLANS

PLATES (*at end*)

LIST OF MAPS

Chapter I

THE DARK AGES

ROMANESQUE Architecture, in its widest sense, may be taken to include all those structural forms which in any way descend from Roman building. Roman building itself was a structural system which borrowed all or nearly all its decorative features, at first or second hand, from the Greeks and was itself responsible only for the general ordinance which resulted from the plan and the structural system. Thus the Byzantine style is in part Romanesque though much of its system and decoration is purely Eastern and its Roman elements have been, in recent years, subjected to a progressive course of subtractive criticism, more and more of its elements being assigned to the East and less and less to Rome. The same critical attack has been made on Roman architecture itself, but without the same success. In this connexion it is not enough to prove that a form of vault or a type of plan was in use, many centuries earlier and many hundreds of miles away, to establish a conscious or unconscious borrowing on the part of the Roman builders. The solution of a structural problem is in no sense analogous to such problems as the unique genesis of the human race, even if that be accepted, and the theory of independent discovery or rediscovery is far more in accord with probability than the supposition that the accomplished Roman engineer or architect took lessons from the amateurish efforts of the brick-builders of the Near or Middle East.

In this wider sense the term Romanesque is in fact curiously inexact as a description of the architecture which prevailed in the western provinces between the fall of Rome and the end of the first millennium; the architecture of this age is normally a reflection, often dim enough, of the church architecture of the age of Constantine and his successors and exhibits little or nothing of the constructive skill which formed the true greatness of Roman work. After the middle of the tenth century, however, there arose a type of building to which the term Romanesque is now more particularly applied and which is in a truer sense derived from Roman structure. Constructive science, which had stood still for five or six centuries in western Europe, began once again to assert itself and with such vigour that it transformed, in the course of two centuries, the solid and stable masses of Roman building into that greatest expression of stone construction— the Gothic structure.

This true Romanesque, as we have said, was preceded by a prolonged period in which architecture, though greatly varied in form, made little or no structural advance. These 'Dark Ages' are themselves divisible into three main epochs, which in most western European countries are sharply divided from one another. These epochs are—the Migration period (4th– 5th century), the first age of the Teutonic kingdoms (6th– 8th century), and finally the Carolingian age (8th–10th century). The Migration period of the Germanic tribes saw the fall of the Western Empire and the establishment of that series of Teutonic kingdoms which form the ground-work of modern Europe. During the actual Migration period, and indeed down to the conversion of the invading races to Christianity, the minor arts of the invaders were of a singularly homogeneous character and their examples can easily be recognized as belonging to that age and culture, whether they be the product of a Gothic, Frankish, Burgundian, Anglo-Saxon, or Lombard deposit. Such building as took place during this period was either in the hands of the subject populations, and as such strictly late Roman, or was timber-structure, like the great hall of Attila (east Hungary), and as such has left no remains.

The second epoch is more germane to our purpose; it covers the Ostrogothic and Lombard periods in Italy, the

Merovingian period in France and Germany, the Visigothic period in Spain, and the period of the Heptarchy in England. In each of these countries the major part of architecture was still almost entirely governed by Roman tradition and it is only in its decoration that the crude beginnings of an individual art begin to make themselves apparent.

It will be well to examine in turn the various countries mentioned above and to note in each the emergence of some form of this incipient national art. It may be premised, in this connexion, that the more Romanized the country the harder was the struggle for new ideas of form and decoration to propagate themselves.

Italy. In Italy the Ostrogothic kingdom of Theodoric the Great (488–526) has bequeathed a few monuments which still survive in the capital city of Ravenna. These, such as the tomb of Theodoric, S. Apollinare Nuovo, and the Arian baptistery, were no doubt due to the direct volition of the Teutonic ruler and his court, but architecturally they are the works of the conquered Italian and only in occasional instances can traces of northern motives be observed. The decoration of Theodoric's tomb has been almost entirely removed, but the upper frieze retains a curious triangle and disk ornament which seems definitely of northern origin. Curiously enough also the three Magi in the mosaics of S. Apollinare Nuovo are represented in barbaric costume, but this is rather the Persian garb, as exemplified in Greek art, than anything distinctly Teutonic.

Between the Ostrogothic and the Lombard supremacies occurs the brilliant episode of Justinian's re-conquest (536 and 552) of Italy. The glories of Ravenna[1] as the capital of the exarchate (539–752) did much for a time to revive the arts in Italy and to create or reinforce the strong Byzantine element in Italian art.

[1] e.g. the churches of S. Vitale, S. Apollinare in Classe, S. Vittore, and the so-called Calchi palace.

The coming and rule of the Lombards (568–774) was almost entirely destructive in its effects, and during their age Italian art sank to the lowest ebb in the whole of its history. The few churches that have survived from that age are largely a patchwork of re-used materials and the stone-mason, when forced to produce a new capital or a decorative feature, only exposed the utter degradation into which his art had fallen. Here and there Italian cities, such as Rome or Milan, kept their heads above the flood and went on producing work in the old tradition but sadly behind the old execution. In the south the Lombard power was not so extensive and the southern Lombard capital, Benevento, even produced works under its northern masters which yet survive. Such are the town-walls and Sta. Sofia, Benevento (Fig. 7); but neither of these bears any trace of northern influence. Towards the close of the period things began to improve and we have at Cividale, the capital of the Lombard duchy of Friuli, a number of monuments of the age. These are the baptistery erected by the Patriarch Callixtus, c. 740, under King Liutprant, and the Pemmo altar (Pl. 1 a) erected by King Ratchis (744–9). Both of these show more or less elaborate interlacements but the figure-subjects on the Pemmo altar are of the crudest description. An even cruder example of Lombard work is to be found in the altar at Ferentillo erected about the middle of the ninth century by a Lombard duke of Foligno, long after the conquest by Charles the Great.

It is an instance of those quaint inversions of which history is full, that it was one of the Lombard kings, Rotharis (636–52), whose code contains the first reference to those associations of masons called the Commacine masters, a reference which has given rise to the wildest theories of the wandering guilds of Lombard masons. The very meaning of the term Commacine is, however, still obscure and the code proves nothing but the bare existence of an organized building craft under the Lombard kings.

Spain. The period of Spanish history which ended with the Moslem invasion and the fall of the Visigothic kingdom at the battle of the Guadalete (711) has left extraordinarily few tangible remains. The most important of these—the votive crowns of Guarrazar—do not concern us, and of all the various structures referred to or described by Isidore of Seville (d. 636) the surviving remains are almost nil. This is the more to be regretted in that the Spanish buildings of the next age are so unusual both in their form and decoration as to imply a different origin from that of the contemporary buildings of Italy. One can only suppose that foreign influence came by way of Africa, for the Visigoths themselves brought with them nothing more than the Ostrogoths or any other Teutonic tribe.

Vicente Lampérez in his monumental work on Spanish Architecture assigns some half a dozen still existing or partly existing buildings to this period, but of these one of the most important—S. Pedro de la Nave—must, in our opinion, be subtracted, as its decoration belongs to a much later date. Of the rest the most important is the church (Fig. 8) of S. Juan de Baños (Palencia), which bears an inscription above the chancel arch recording its erection by King Recesvint in 661. This church provides an early example of a number of features which distinguished some Spanish church-building of the next period. The most important of these is the use of the horseshoe arch, which there seems no reason to doubt was distinctive of the Visigothic builders, as it appears in a number of stelae (Pl. 4 *a*) and memorial stones which are definitely dated either within the period or before it and thus antedate any appearance of the horseshoe arch in Islamic architecture, and indeed antedate Islam itself. The church furthermore has the square east end which is the usual form in the succeeding period. As to the chambers flanking the church and their eastern annexes, of which the foundations have been uncovered, they seem to be a local form of those subsidiary 'porticus' which are familiar to us in our own English churches of the same age. The other important surviving churches are of more special type; that at Sta. Comba de Bande (Orense) is of Greek cross form, while that at S. Miguel de Tarrasa (Barcelona) is a baptistery (built between 450 and 720) of a form common in structures of this character. The roofs of the chancel at Baños and of the four arms at Bande are of barrel-form, which is the only form of vault in use in the English churches of the same age.

The column-capitals of this age are, as might be expected, of classical or semi-classical Corinthian form, but the minor ornament is more significant. It consists largely of a geometrical application of the wood-technique known as chip-carving, and no doubt is to be derived from a wooden original. This may be seen on some of the stelae above mentioned, on a window-head at Merida, and on an altar and other fragments at Cordova. A fragment with eastern decoration of confronted beasts, foliage, and horseshoe arches is preserved at Lisbon Cathedral (Pl. 2 a).

Before leaving the subject attention may be called to a building erected by the Visigothic kings while they were seated at Toulouse, and which survived until the eighteenth century. This was the church of our Lady at Toulouse, called from the golden ground of its mosaics the Daurade. It was a decagon on plan, lit by a central opening in the dome (like the Pantheon at Rome), and must have been the work of Latin or Greek craftsmen.

Gaul and Germany. Merovingian building in France is confined to a comparatively small number of structures, almost all of which are of special character such as crypts and baptisteries. We know comparatively little of the form of the major or minor churches of this age save what can be gathered from the descriptions of Gregory of Tours. From them and from the foundations of the early churches at S. Denis and elsewhere it would appear that the major churches

followed the general lines of the early Christian buildings of
Rome and Italy and sometimes adopted the T-cross type of
plan. Of the smaller churches only fragments have survived
(Fig. 3). Poitiers is rich in possessing two undoubted Merovingian buildings in the baptistery and the Hypogeum. The
former (Pl. 5 b) is of unique form but has been much altered
at later dates; the latter is a chapel erected c. 600 over the
remains of the early martyrs of Poitiers, and was no doubt
destroyed by the Saracens before their defeat at Tours in 732.
Other buildings of the same age are the baptistery at Venas-
que, and the crypts at St. Laurent, Grenoble, and at Jouarre.

The ornament of these buildings is somewhat enigmatical,
for while the column-capitals, such as those at Jouarre, sometimes exhibit a high degree of proficiency and even an occasional innovation on the purely classical form, the other
decoration is often of the crudest character. The carvings of
the Hypogeum at Poitiers are a case in point; the figures here
are on a par artistically with those of the Lombard carvers
already referred to and the other ornament is of little higher
quality. It must be recognized, however, that the standard
of work in the south is consistently higher than that in the
north, the Latin civilization of the south not having suffered
the clean sweep that it was subject to in the northern part of
the country. The ornament of the Hypogeum (Pl. 2 b) forms
a safely dated if not very extensive corpus of Merovingian
ornament. It includes crude interlacement, ivy-vine ornament, and rosettes of various forms and shows a very marked
decadence from the ornament of sarcophagi from southern
France of fifty to a hundred years earlier. The same rosette
ornament is to be seen on some of the sarcophagi at Jouarre.
Another feature that may be noticed is the pronounced
herring-bone or diagonal tooling within panels to be found on
the surface of otherwise plain Merovingian sarcophagi from
Ste. Geneviève, Paris (Musée Carnavalet), the Hypogeum,
and some recently discovered under the minster at Bonn.

Germany is poor in remains of this age, the early buildings being nearly all either of late Roman date or verging on the Carolingian period. Mention, however, may be made of parts of the round church on the Festamarienburg at Würzburg, which was built in 706 and is a direct copy of a Roman type. Foundations have also been discovered of the early church (744–54) at Fulda and of two small eighth-century churches at Hersfeld.[1]

England. Early Anglo-Saxon building of the period of the Heptarchy is derived from two sources. The southern group of churches is of direct Italian inspiration, due to the Roman missions of St. Augustine and St. Theodore; these churches are mostly in Kent and remains of some half a dozen have been found by excavation or still survive. They are distinguished by a simple aisle-less plan with an apsidal chancel and a series of annexes called 'porticus' adjoining or surrounding the nave. The most complete plan yet recovered is that of the church at Reculver (Fig. 5) founded in 669 and added to during the following century. An advance on this type is to be found at Brixworth (Pl. 3 *b*), founded probably late in the seventh century and still largely surviving. It is an aisled basilica with arcades and windows built in the Roman fashion. An almost universal feature of this group is the three-arched opening between the nave and the chancel, which may be paralleled in both Italy and north Africa at an earlier date. The northern group of churches built under the influence of St. Benedict Biscop and St. Wilfrid should, according to the literary evidence, be derived from Merovingian Gaul, but no certain church of the age has survived at all complete and the theory must remain unproven.

The decoration of these churches and more particularly of the standing stone crosses (Pl. 4 *b*) of the age exhibits a curious and elsewhere unparalleled outbreak of decorative art of a high order. Derived ultimately from the East the

[1] *Fuldaer Geschichts-Verein,* xvi (1919) and xvii (1924).

immediate sources of this art are so far unexplained, though the mission of St. Theodore, a Greek by birth, forms a tempting setting. The Syrian vine-scroll with birds and beasts occupies the most prominent place in this decoration, but it is accompanied by elaborate interlacement and a revival of certain Celtic motives such as the trumpet-spiral, together with some animal forms directly of Teutonic and ultimately of Scythian origin.

THE CAROLINGIAN RENAISSANCE

The revival of Roman art and learning under Charles the Great was an effort in which only the extraordinary personality of the emperor and his long reign (768–814) enabled him to achieve a measure of success. The idea of uniting the revival of the political structure of the Western Empire with a corresponding revival of its civilization was a titanic conception to which the times allowed only a partial realization. The unlearned emperor succeeded in a remarkable degree in re-establishing not only learning but also some of the minor arts such as illumination and ivory carving; nevertheless in the major art of architecture his success was of more doubtful quality. The direct copying of certain Italian forms and even the actual importation of antique materials across the Alps could give only a veneer of classical polish to an art which was essentially in the hands of the unlettered local craftsmen. Thus, although important buildings sprang up throughout Charles's empire, they are the local product of a flourishing age and resemble only remotely the early churches of Rome and Italy.

In general plan the Carolingian churches exhibit a great advance on the simple arrangements of the preceding age. The transept, instead of being confined to a few major churches, now becomes the rule rather than the exception. More important than this, however, is the equal importance assigned to the two ends of the church, of which the most marked expression is in the double-apse plan. It has been suggested that this unusual plan was primarily adopted to serve the purposes of those double monasteries which were common in this and the preceding age, the eastern apse and choir being used by the monks and the west apse and choir by the nuns of the mixed community. This theory is to a certain extent supported by the continued use of the western nuns' choir, at any rate in name, down to a far later period in Germany. The earliest double-apse plan in western Europe of which evidence has survived is that recorded to have existed at Abingdon (Berks.) in the seventh century. The form, however, only became frequent in the Carolingian age, when it was adopted in the celebrated plan of St. Gall, at Cologne Cathedral, at Fulda, and at numerous other places, and so impressed itself on the Rhineland that it persisted there far into the Middle Ages. The western apse was, however, by no means universal; in many churches the west choir was accommodated in a square west end or set upon a west gallery so as to allow free entrance beneath it by the west front. The use of the double-ended church also brought with it that of the double transept, the crossing of both being often crowned by those many staged square or polygonal towers, which if not the creation of the Carolingian architects were at any rate brought to perfection by them. Many of the Carolingian churches furthermore had a deeply projecting chancel, a definite advance on the early Christian type, with only the apse projecting east from the tau-shaped plan. The earlier plan, however, was preserved in a number of cases of which the second church at Fulda, the two churches of Einhard, Charles's minister, at Michelstadt and Seligenstadt in the Odenwald, and the church on the Heiligenberg (near Heidelberg) are prominent examples.

A notable survival from an earlier age is the arcaded fore-court or atrium which is by no means infrequent in the larger Carolingian buildings and survived in Germany as late as the twelfth century. The exterior of these churches no doubt owed much of its individuality to the extensive and frequent use of the cylindrical staircase towers, generally set in pairs towards the east and west ends of the building.

The minster at Aachen (Pl. 6 a and Fig. 10), the most noted structure of the age, built by Charles the Great as a palace-chapel and tomb-house, was a revival of an ancient form, and seeing that some of its fittings were imported from Ravenna there seems no reason to doubt that its general features were an attempted copy of the sixth-century church of S. Vitale there. That this copy fell far below the original need hardly be said, but nevertheless the minster at Aachen was no mean achievement for its age. It consists of a four-storied central structure of octagonal form surmounted by an octagonal dome, and round it runs a two-storied ambulatory with groined vaults over the lower story. On the west side is a tower porch with two cylindrical stair-turrets and on the east was a square altar projection, now destroyed. That Aachen minster greatly impressed the men of its own and later ages is proved by the continued copying of its form in later buildings.

Stone vaulting in the Carolingian age was, however, confined to such special buildings, to crypts and to apses; the normal church was otherwise completely timber-roofed in conformity with early Christian tradition. The general structure of these buildings was severely plain; square piers supported simple round arches, high above which ran a clerestory of round-headed windows. North of the Alps the use of columns for the arcades is highly unusual, there being little or no local supply of antique columns and the importation of these from Italy being possible to few save the emperor himself. The masonry often displays the use of brick bands or cordons, a use which was unbroken from the Roman period, and the external surfaces are sometimes treated in a highly decorative manner by the use of polychrome materials, pyramidal designs, and the ornamental setting of the individual facing stones. The simple construction of a normal Carolingian church can still be studied in the remains of Einhard's two churches mentioned above and in a few still surviving churches on or near the Lake of Constance and including Reichenau.

Churches of the type described in a summary manner above are common to the essential part of Charles's empire, the old Frankish kingdoms Austrasia and Neustria (south-west Germany and north France). The influence of his revival of the arts was, however, much more extensive and made itself felt in southern France, Italy, and England, and even in some small degree in northern Spain.

In Germany parts of many surviving buildings have by one or another author been ascribed to the Carolingian age, and though many of these will not bear a close investigation yet a considerable number may be considered as still possessing important structural survivals from this age. Two important groups in the Odenwald and in the Constance district have already been noted and a large number more in a fragmentary state might be cited. One of the most important of these is the west building[1] called the Peterskirche at Werden a. d. Ruhr built in the first third of the tenth century. It consists of a very large central tower with barrel-vaulted annexes on three sides. The minster at Aachen had a counterpart at Nijmwegen (Holland), largely rebuilt in the twelfth century, and a series of more or less close copies elsewhere.

One structure deserves a more lengthy consideration as its date has occasioned acute controversy; this is the Torhalle (Pl. 5 a) at Lorsch (near Worms). The abbey was founded in 764 and the church consecrated in 774. The church was destroyed by fire in 1090 and rebuilt, the new church being consecrated in 1130. The existing remarkable building stood isolated in the middle of the forecourt;[2] it is attributed by

[1] Compare also the earlier west building at Korvey (873–85).
[2] The foundations of the original lay-out were uncovered in 1927. F. Behn in *Zeitschrift f. Denkmalpflege*, iii (1928–9), p. 20.

most German writers to the late eighth-century building but is assigned by Lasteyrie to the period of the twelfth-century structure, on the grounds that its detail is far finer than that of the minster at Aachen and that its individual characteristics can be paralleled in twelfth-century building in France. Had this author produced parallels in twelfth-century Germany his arguments would have had greater weight. As it is, there seems no reason to suppose that the Torhalle was contemporary with the first church; it might well have been built fifty or a hundred years later. There is no doubt that its general scheme of decoration accords much better with the Carolingian than with any later period and most of its details[1] can be paralleled in work of that age.

The surviving remains of Carolingian buildings in France are less important than those of Germany. We have, however, the important church of S. Philbert de Grandlieu (Fig. 4), built *c.* 819 and subsequently enlarged and altered, S. Martin of Angers, much of the structure of S. Pierre, Vienne, and S. Aphrodise, Béziers, and a number of minor buildings such as Germigny-des-Prés (Pl. 6 *b* and Fig. 11), Cravant, S. Généreux, S. Pierre, Jumièges, &c., which are important examples of Carolingian ornament.

If, however, the structural remains of Carolingian churches are comparatively few in number it is otherwise with the debris of their carved decoration, which is scattered freely not only over France and Germany but also over northern Italy. These remains consist of carved panels from screens, ambos, altar-canopies, sarcophagi, &c., and display a very general uniformity of *motif.* The repeating designs or diapering consist of various forms of interlacement, scrolled foliage, or a particular variety of the vine-scroll which is commonly distinguished by the use of a seed-pod form of grape-cluster. This last makes its appearance in Italy about the beginning

---

[1] The composite capitals of the front may be compared with those from the Carolingian palace at Ingelheim.

of the ninth century and is as widely spread as Spain, Italy, and England. The Carolingian crocket makes its appearance in the second half of the eighth century and is equally widely diffused. Figure-carving, in stone, is but little used, and when it does appear shows little advance on that of the previous age; the relief is very flat, the form bad, and the drawing indicated by shallow grooves.

The Carolingian artists, on the other hand, made extensive use of plaster and stucco decoration. The few surviving examples of this medium are but a poor indication of its former importance, which is fully attested by documentary sources.[1] Remains of elaborate decoration in this material survive at Cividale, Mals, Germigny-des-Prés, and elsewhere, and this is accompanied at Cividale by a series of full-length figures in high relief (Pl. 1 b) which give some idea of the importance that such decoration might assume. It should be noted that the date of the stuccoes at Cividale is much disputed, various authorities placing them as far apart as the eighth and the twelfth century. The Tempietto (Fig. 1), in which they are placed, however, forms part of a building founded in the eighth century and the decorative scheme of the naturalistic vine-scroll would be very difficult to parallel in twelfth-century Italy. The excellence of the work is really the stumbling-block; it still seems impossible for most authors to allow that anything good came from the centuries before the twelfth, an attitude which is becoming more and more unsupported by the known facts. We really know so little about Carolingian figure-modelling in plaster that it is in the highest degree dangerous to dogmatize as to what was or was not possible in this medium. We know, at least, that large figure-subjects were executed in stucco covering great stretches of wall-surface (such were the Crucifixion, Nativity, and Resurrection at S. Riquier) and it is impossible to conceive such subjects executed on the artistic level of contemporary stone carving.

[1] e.g. S. Riquier, described below.

Church-fittings in metal of this age are obviously a still more infrequent survival; mention, however, may be made of the altar-frontal of S. Ambrogio, Milan, executed by Volvignus for Archbishop Angilbert in the ninth century and covered with small scenes in relief which testify to a metal-working art approaching that of the ivory-carvers.

We have so far dealt with the buildings of the age only in purely Carolingian lands; to complete our résumé it will be necessary to pass rapidly in review the state of the building-art in countries not immediately controlled by the Carolingian revival.

Italy, though part of the political empire, owed little herself to this revival which indeed drew most of its inspiration from within her borders. The Italian buildings of the age show little or no inclination towards change either in plan or structure. In plan the only innovation seems to be the introduction of side apses forming a tri-apsidal termination to the building. This first appears at Sta. Maria in Cosmedin, Rome (772–95). Bell-towers began first to assume importance at this period and were added, in a somewhat haphazard manner, to many earlier structures. Though the great majority were square, the round form also appears at this time at Ravenna, and Ricci assumes that its origin was due to the fact that the earliest was raised after 910 on one of the round staircases at S. Vitale. It was imitated at S. Apollinare Nuovo after 973 and there were eventually nine towers of this form in the city. It seems more probable that the adoption of the round form was copied from the northern Carolingian staircase-towers, which appear at a much earlier date.

Spain. The architecture of the early Christian kingdoms, lying along the northern seaboard, where the broken remnants of Visigothic power preserved their independence and gradually increased their territory at the expense of the Islamic states, forms one of the most remarkable episodes in European art-history. Largely cut off, at any rate for the first two centuries of their existence, from intercourse with the outside world, they developed a highly individual type of building which has only occasional points of contact with those of the rest of Europe and though these structures are perhaps authenticated chronologically as well as or better than any other group of buildings elsewhere, their claims to such antiquity have been resolutely denied, particularly by the earlier French authors. There seems to be not the slightest reason for this scepticism save that the structure of these Spanish churches is greatly in advance of the contemporary buildings of France and was consequently highly suspect in Gallic eyes. On the other hand the very unusual form of the buildings would render them entirely out of place at any later date, and their decoration, often elaborate enough, is completely in accord with their attribution to the eighth, ninth, and tenth centuries. In general these Asturian churches are of small dimensions, but show a highly developed plan which is sometimes cruciform and is invariably accompanied by a series of symmetrically disposed chapels or porticus. These chapels and chambers often flank the two ends of the building but also appear in the form of transepts. The free use of barrel-vaulting, reinforced in the later examples by ribs, carries with it the equally free use of buttresses of almost Gothic projection, which is one of the distinctive features of the Spanish churches of this age. There is furthermore an almost universal use of the square east end, both to the chancel and chapels, which is only abandoned in certain churches built for the Christians still under Moslem dominion or for those driven out by the persecution of Abderrahman II in the first half of the ninth century. These Mozarabic churches retained the use of the horseshoe arch, inherited from the Visigoths and generally adopted by the Moors, whereas this form is almost entirely absent from the purely Asturian churches.

The earliest surviving Asturian church seems to be S. Juan de Pravia (Santiañes) built by King Silo (774–83). Here the barrel-vault is confined to the chancel and consequently no buttresses are needed. Pravia at this time became the royal seat and in the vestibule of the church are several royal tombs. The next group is either in or near the city of Oviedo, where three churches were built by Alfonso II the Chaste (791–842). Of these only a part of the Camara Santa (*c.* 802) survives, but the church of S. Julián de los Prados outside the wall still exists and here buttresses make their appearance. Near Oviedo are the two remarkable churches of S. Miguel de Liño (founded by Ramiro I in 848) and Sta. Maria de Naranco (dedicated in 848). Both of these buildings have a complete system of barrel-vaulting and the second (Pl. 3 *a*) is remarkable also for its unusual plan. This is an oblong apartment opening by three arches at each end into a narthex. This arrangement has led to the theory that the structure was built as the hall of the palace which Ramiro is known to have built in the neighbourhood. On the other hand, the inscription on the altar records that Ramiro renovated this 'habitaculum', almost destroyed by age. Other churches of the same general type are Sta. Cristina de Lena (Fig. 9) (first quarter tenth century), S. Salvador de Valdediós (*c.* 893), S. Salvador de Priesca (*c.* 921), and in all probability S. Pedro de la Nave (Zamora), which in form and decoration belongs much more closely to this period (893–907) than to the Visigothic to which Señor Gómez-Moreno seeks to ascribe it.

The carved decoration of these churches is much more extensive and elaborate than is usual in Carolingian churches elsewhere. The Visigothic rosettes and crosses in circles still survive and are accompanied very commonly by the seed-pod vine-scroll we have already noted, but though these motives occur as elsewhere on screens and other fittings, in Spain they are used also as architectural decorations. They form a continuous band or string-course at S. Pedro de la Nave and are repeated on the deep abaci of the responds. A similar use is made of them on archivolts at S. Miguel de Liño. At the same place the jambs of the doorway are formed of carved slabs with figure-subjects and a broad bay-leaf border; this has been identified as a direct copy on a larger scale of the leaf of a consular diptych showing combats in the arena. Almost equally unusual are the remarkable decorations below the cross-ribs of the vault at Sta. Maria de Naranco; these take the form of a modern medal and ribbon, the ribbon being carved with crude figures and the medallion with beasts and a foliage border. The columns, border, and mouldings show a free use of the cable *motif*, and the capitals when not adhering to the Corinthian tradition are highly varied both in their form and decoration.

It is interesting to compare this decoration with the perfect execution of the pure Byzantine capitals and other ornament of the Umayyad palace at Medina az Zahra and other buildings in and near Cordova. The comparison will serve to show how little the high standard of work in the western Caliphate affected contemporary architecture in the Christian north.

That this architecture has some connexion with Italy is proved not only by the introduction of the seed-pod vine but also by certain striking analogies between the form of the Tempietto at Cividale and that of some of the Asturian churches; the use of the triple arcade is a notable equation, and the plan has other features in common. On the other hand, the differences far outweigh the equations, and Asturian architecture would seem to be in great part a native growth which was unfortunately entirely blotted out by the imported Romanesque style of the succeeding period.

England. The documentary evidence relating to the greater English churches of the period succeeding the Danish invasions seems sufficient to show that, in their main lines, they followed the course of the continental Carolingian style. Unfortunately they have without exception perished, and the ruins at North Elmham (Fig. 6) form the only survival which gives us any idea of what an Anglo-Saxon cathedral was like.

Here the tau-cross plan was adopted with an arrangement of towers not unlike that of some of the German churches—two minor ones in the angle of the transept and a major one at the west end; this last has a broad arch opening into it and may well have contained a west choir and gallery. The smaller churches preserved some of the features of the previous age, but the flanking porticus of the early period tend more and more to become transepts. Many of these churches, such as Deerhurst, Dover (St. Mary in Castro), Bosham, &c., retain evidence of west galleries, no doubt used as western choirs as in the continental Carolingian churches. The most notable feature of the surviving English churches of the age is the tower. Many of these are of a scale and importance apparently out of proportion to the church to which they were annexed. The towers of Earl's Barton, Barnack, and Clapham are well-known instances. There is documentary evidence that several of the greater churches were provided with two main towers set axially over the crossing and the west end of the church, and this practice was one of the few that left its impress on English post-Conquest architecture.

Structurally the English churches were no farther advanced than the Carolingian churches of the continent; vaulting was used only in crypts, for the few later Saxon apses were commonly polygonal (e.g. Deerhurst and Wing) and hence unsuited to the semi-domed vault then in use. In structural decoration also this architecture was singularly unambitious. Here and there are remains of large sculptural subjects mostly in stone but sometimes so incomplete as to imply that the subject was partly in stucco. Late Anglo-Saxon ornament, however, falls far below the standard of the earlier age, and in the later standing crosses, tomb-slabs, and isolated carvings we see only the degraded tradition of the earlier age or the infiltration of Scandinavian art. In figure-sculpture there was, however, a late revival which will be considered in connexion with the Ottonian revival in Germany.

SUMMARY BIBLIOGRAPHY

GENERAL WORKS.

A. Haupt, *Die älteste Kunst insbesondere die Baukunst der Germanen*, 1909.

Dehio u. von Bezold, *Kirchliche Baukunst des Abendlandes*, 1884–1901.

R. Hinks, *Carolingian Art*, 1935.

ITALY.

R. Cattaneo, *Architecture in Italy from the Sixth to the Eleventh Century*, 1896.

G. T. Rivoira, *Lombardic Architecture*, 2nd ed., 1933.

A. Haseloff, *Die vorromanische Plastik in Italien*, 1930.

FRANCE.

R. de Lasteyrie, *Architecture religieuse en France à l'époque romane*, 2nd ed., 1929.

GERMANY.

E. Gall, *Karolingische und ottonische Kirchen* (Deutsche Bauten), 1930.

SPAIN.

V. Lampérez, *Arquitectura cristiana española en la edad media*, vol. i, 2nd ed., 1930.

M. Gómez-Moveno, *Iglesías mozárabes*, 1919.

ENGLAND.

Baldwin Brown, *The Arts in Early England*, vol. ii, Architecture, 2nd ed., 1925.

A. W. Clapham, *English Romanesque Architecture before the Conquest*, 1930.

Chapter II

FIRST ROMANESQUE ARCHITECTURE

THE term 'first Romanesque art' has been invented and applied by Señor Puig[1] to a widely diffused type of building of which he has traced the origin and extent and which he rightly considers the immediate precursor of the full Romanesque style.

Following Quicherat he considers that 'the vault, considered in its form, in its outline and in its economy, is always the essential feature of Romanesque architecture; apart from the general lines of the plan and the free fancy of the decoration, everything is subordinated to it'. The rise of Romanesque, considered in this light, may be said to be in great part due to the troubles and disasters which overtook western Europe during the decline and fall of the Carolingian dynasty. The almost universal incursions of the Normans with their accompanying pillage and destruction, either threatened or overtook almost every church which had anything worth the looting. Repeated disasters formed a very pressing and cogent motive for the production of a form of structure at once more solid and less destructible than that which had held the field since the age of Constantine. That such was the immediate motive for the change in structure in Catalonia is proved by a number of instances cited by Señor Puig in which the burning of a church, in this case by the Moors, was followed by its rebuilding in a form that was unburnable, the wooden roofs of the earlier building being replaced by the stone vaults of the later structure. There seems little reason to doubt that the return to this use of the stone vault made its first beginnings in those provinces where extensive survivals of Roman imperial building provided an object lesson which the needs of the age forced the Romanesque

[1] J. Puig y Cadafalch, *Le premier art roman*, 1928.

builders to apply. It was thus in northern Italy, on the shores of the Gulf of Lyons, and in the Rhone valley that the first Romanesque art took its rise. At first the use of vaulting was confined to a narrow bay before the apse, and an attempt was made to retain the earlier columned form of the nave. Soon, however, the column gave place to the pier, and though in northern Italy the wooden roof died hard, elsewhere the completely vaulted church became the rule and not the exception. The rise of the new style was marked by a great outburst of building activity, in the districts above mentioned, in the latter part of the tenth and the early part of the succeeding century; this is the revival of church-building attributed by Raoul Glaber to the passing of the fated year 1000, but which in fact began a generation or more earlier.

That the new style first emerged in northern Italy is indicated by the fact that the earliest surviving churches, displaying its distinctive features, are to be found in that district and that they antedate the appearance of the type elsewhere by a century or so. This early appearance in Lombardy, with some reason, led earlier writers to label the style Lombardic, but since in its earlier expression it extended far beyond Lombardy and achieved its greatest results elsewhere it is preferable on the whole to adhere to the new name of first Romanesque.

The earlier examples of the new type are commonly aisled basilicas, only differing from the older churches by the presence of two side-apses at the east end and by the introduction of a narrow vaulted bay between the main apse and the nave. Apart from this bay and the three apses the earlier churches retained the traditional timber roof. The walls are built throughout of rubble and the windows are commonly of the type called double-splayed, that is to say, with the glass or shutter-line in the centre of the wall and the jambs splayed equally inside and out. This form of window distinguishes the contemporary work in England. The arches are of simple rounded form without decoration and often spring from the supporting pier without the interposition of either capital or impost.

It is, however, the external ornament of these buildings which gives them the distinctive appearance which is popularly connected with the Lombard style. This ornament is of the simplest character and consists of the division of the wall-surface into bays by vertical bands or pilasters of slight projection, and extending nearly to the full height of the wall. At the top they form the apparent support of a range of shallow round arches under the eaves and forming a sort of deep cornice. Where this decoration is applied to a tower the arcaded horizontal bands are introduced to mark the divisions into stages, and a lofty wall-surface is often treated in the same manner. The place of the series of arches is sometimes taken by a corresponding series of recesses, not pierced through the wall, but having a sloping sill and sufficiently deep to cast a heavy shadow. The shallow arcading at the head of a wall was not a new invention of the Lombard builders; it had appeared centuries before in such buildings as the orthodox baptistry at Ravenna, but the tradition appears to have been entirely broken in the interval.

There can be little doubt that these early structures were plastered and limewashed both within and without, and in addition to this they may well have received a stucco decoration of the type then current in Carolingian churches and to which we have referred above. In the early examples at any rate there is no trace of structural ornament in any more durable material, while portions of stucco ornament have, here and there, survived.

The earliest north Italian church in which all the distinctive features of the new style make a simultaneous appearance is at Agliate (S. Pietro), near Monza, where the structure (Pl. 7 a, Fig. 15) is safely dated to about the year 875. The niched recesses of the apse are repeated in a number of Milanese churches of about the same or a rather later period, of which the east end of S. Ambrogio (*c*. 940) is the best known. The bay between the apse and the nave at Agliate is covered by a barrel-vault, while the corresponding bays in the side aisles have groined vaults. Professor Kingsley Porter has collected a whole series of churches of this type in Lombardy extending from the ninth to the end of the eleventh century in which little advance is observable in some churches, either in roof-covering or in the form of the pier, whereas in others the whole system of construction has been revolutionized and the groined vault has given place to a primitive form of ribbed vault before the end of the eleventh century. This development, however, belongs properly to the next period and must not be considered here.

There seems little doubt that the new style was transmitted along the shores of the Gulf of Lyons to Catalonia, where there survives a remarkably complete series of examples showing every stage of the evolution from the timber-roofed building to the completely vaulted one. Externally they are, many of them, indistinguishable from those of the north Italian group, but the Catalonian builders proved in some respects more enterprising than the Italian, and both here and in southern France arose a number of churches of great variety in plan and often eclipsing in size the churches of the Lombard group. The earliest Catalonian churches of the type appear about the middle of the tenth century and are preceded by a small group of Mozarabic churches from which they are sharply divided both in type and structure. The most obvious distinction is the retention, in the earlier buildings, of the horseshoe arch, the adoption of which we have seen is distinctive of the Mozarabic buildings and which is entirely abandoned in the first Romanesque style. A few early churches of the Lombard type retain the wooden roofs of their early Italian prototypes, but this was soon generally abandoned in favour of the completely vaulted church. The earliest dated examples appear to be Sta. Maria d'Amer, 949,

and Sta. Cecilia de Montserrat, 957, though the church of
L'Ecluse may be slightly more ancient. In all these examples
the nave and aisles either are or were covered by continuous
barrel-vaults, the middle vault being slightly higher than the
others.

The next advance was the re-enforcing of the barrel-vault
by cross-ribs or arches between each bay. This improvement
is to be seen at S. Pedro de Casserres (c. 1010) and at a later
date in the neighbouring French churches of Arles-sur-Tech
(1046) and Elne Cathedral (1042–68). The adoption of the
cross-ribs was accompanied by the use of the cruciform or
compound pier to provide a direct support for the arches
springing in the four directions. In a small number of
churches in France and Aragon the barrel-vaults are replaced
by a system of groined vaults.

Two further developments remain to be noticed—the introduction of the cupola or dome and that of the cruciform plan.
The two often appear in conjunction, but it appears likely that
the cruciform plan with deeply projecting arms appeared before the adoption of the central cupola. Although occasionally,
as at the abbey of Ripoll (1032), the transept is of the T-
form of the earlier ages, more generally the arrangement
takes the Latin-cross form distinctive of the full Romanesque style. Furthermore, these cruciform churches are largely
confined to France and Catalonia and never became popular
in Lombardy.

According to Kingsley Porter the earliest Lombard church
with a surviving cupola is the cathedral of Acqui, begun
about 1000 and largely finished by 1042. In Catalonia the
important church of S. Vicente de Cardona (1020–40), apart
from the introduction of the cupola, makes a very definite
advance in that the main roof rises sufficiently highly above
the groined vaults of the side aisles to allow of a clerestory
to light the nave. In France the earliest church of the
type provided with a transept and central cupola is S. Vorles,

Châtillon-sur-Seine (Pl. 8 *a*, and Fig. 17), which would appear to have been built about 991.

This later development of the cruciform plan produced in south France and north-east Spain a highly remarkable series of churches which are distinguished by a variety in plan, construction, and general outline, which are perhaps unparalleled at any other age and indicate the extreme activity and inventiveness of mind which characterized the builders of the age. To obtain some idea of this very fecund architectural expression it will be desirable to pass in review a few of the principal constructions in which it is displayed.

We have already touched upon the great church at Ripoll built by Abbot Oliva and consecrated 1032. The builder was described at his death as 'animator of things ecclesiastical and of buildings of admirable structure'. The church at Ripoll (Pl. 10 *a*, and Fig. 16) is the most important monument of its age in Catalonia but is in many points conservative in its type; indeed it would seem that the builder desired to reproduce in the Pyrenean monastery a copy of the great basilica of St. Peter at Rome. There are the same five aisles to the nave, the tau-cross plan, and the seven apses projecting to the east. The contemporary church of S. Vicente de Cardona (Pl. 10 *b*), built between 1020 and 1040, is, on the other hand, of the fully developed Romanesque plan, with small apses east of the transept and an apsidal choir. The choir is enriched within by a series of apsidal recesses, forming a continuous wall-arcade. In the Rousillon, north of the Pyrenees, are the two remarkable abbey-churches of S. Michel de Cuxa and S. Martin du Canigou. The former (Pl. 8 *b*, and Fig. 14), consecrated in 974 and enlarged *c*. 1020, had a square eastern ambulatory and seven apsidal chapels to this and the transept. The two arms of the transept terminated in massive square towers, one of which still survives. At the west end was a narthex and a round structure, somewhat similar in general arrangement to the early baptistery at Fréjus and evidently inspired by some such early model. Canigou still retains the plan without a transept and stands on an extensive crypt; many of its peculiarities, however, are due to its situation perched on a rock.

In the Rhône basin two churches demand attention, Tournus and S. Bénigne at Dijon. Tournus, built by monks driven from the island-monastery of Noirmoutier, near the mouth of the Loire, by the Norman raids, is a highly remarkable building, which has perhaps aroused more discussion than any other single church in France. No finality has yet been arrived at, but there seems to be a general agreement that the crypt was built and finished in 979 when the body of the patron S. Philibert was transferred to it, and that the vast narthex (Pl. 9) was an addition of only slightly later date, perhaps about 1000. The acceptance of these dates carries with it the adoption of a fully developed ambulatory plan with radiating chapels in the last quarter of the tenth century, for this is the plan of the crypt, and the lower part of the choir above may be partly of the same date. This type of plan appeared yet earlier in the crypt of Clermont-Ferrand cathedral, built 946, but its ultimate origin is not yet explained. The narthex at Tournus is in every way a remarkable structure; it consists of two stories exhibiting no less than three types of vault—the groined vault in the middle nave of the ground story, the barrel vault in the aisles and the main body of the upper story, and supported by half barrel-vaults over the side aisles. The church of S. Bénigne at Dijon consisted of a large five-aisled basilica, now completely disappeared, a vast rotunda, with double aisles, to the east of it, and a rectangular chapel still farther east. The basilica and the rotunda, built 1001–17, were both the work of St. William of Volpiano, an Italian, trained at Cluny, who reformed the abbey of S. Bénigne and was subsequently called in to reform the abbeys of the north of France. The lower story of the rotunda and of the eastern chapel alone survive, but drawings

of the complete rotunda, before its destruction in 1792, show
on what ambitious lines it was conceived. It appears to have
served as the model for the remarkable structure built by
Abbot Wulfric at St. Augustine's, Canterbury, about the
middle of the eleventh century. Lastly, we may note the
church of S. Vorles, Châtillon-sur-Seine, which, though of
modest dimensions, is fairly well preserved and has a remarkable feature in its west transept which may well have been
adopted from Carolingian models. There seems little reason
to doubt the ascription of this church to the date 991
generally assigned to it.

Throughout all these churches we encounter the distinguishing features, both in structure and in the ornamental use,
of the so-called Lombard bands and wall-arcading which are
distinctive of the first Romanesque style, and we must now
consider how far this style extended. The investigations of
Señor Puig have established its predominance throughout
Lombardy, the sea-board of the Gulf of Lyons, Catalonia,
and the basin of the Rhône and Saone. Beyond these limits
it penetrated but partially or not at all. Thus there is no
evidence that it passed the watershed of the Rhône and the
Loire, though, as we have seen at Châtillon, it makes a single
appearance at the head-waters of the Seine. Elsewhere in
north and north-western France it is entirely unrepresented.
It passed, however, into Switzerland and thence in isolated
examples into Germany and the Low Countries. Thus we
find a few eleventh-century village churches in Switzerland,[1]
such as Amsoldingen and Spiez, exhibiting nearly all of the
salient characteristics of the style, but in Germany generally
the Carolingian tradition was too strong for it to obtain more
than a foothold. In Lombardy and north Italy generally the
style developed normally and gradually into the full Lombardic Romanesque and this was in due course transmitted to

---

[1] M. Grätter, 'Die romanischen Kirchen am Thunersee', in *Anzeiger
für schweizerische Altertumskunde*, xxxiv (1932).

Germany, the Low Countries, and Scandinavia, but elsewhere the tradition was lost in the rise of the more vital Romanesque styles of central and southern France and the Lombardic style, in its later development, makes only an occasional appearance in such buildings as the towers of Arles and Uzès cathedrals, the Manécanterie at Lyon, and elsewhere.

SUMMARY BIBLIOGRAPHY

J. Puig y Cadafalch, *Le premier art roman*, 1928.
———— *La Geografia i els Orígens del primer Art romànic*, 1930.

Chapter III

ITALY, SICILY, AND DALMATIA

WE have traced in the early part of the previous chapter the rise of the first Romanesque or early Lombard style in northern Italy and its rapid expansion over south-eastern France, Catalonia, and parts of central Europe. Its further and fuller development in northern Italy must now engage our attention, for not only was it the most vital expression of Italian Romanesque but it formed one of the main inspirations of Romanesque architecture in Germany, Scandinavia, Hungary, and Dalmatia. The style is native to the provinces of Lombardy, Piedmont, Emilia, and parts of Venetia, and may be said to be centred in Milan and the old Lombard capital Pavia. Tuscany, on the other hand, developed rather on lines of its own, centred at Pisa, Florence, and Lucca, while Rome held firmly to its classical traditions and only grudgingly admitted a few expressions of what may be termed Romanesque art. Southern Italy, artistically, was largely cut off from the northern half of the country and its Romanesque, touched here with Lombard and there with Pisan influence, is essentially different from either.

The first Romanesque buildings are distinguished, as we have seen, by a return to the general use of the stone vault, which was necessarily preceded by the substitution of the pier-arcade for the column-arcade, the latter being structurally quite unsuited to the support of a stone vault. In Italy the column-basilica proved very difficult to supplant, largely because of the almost inexhaustible supply of antique columns, which led often to their incongruous use in an otherwise purely Romanesque building. Stone-vaulting, either of the groined or barrel form, had also never been entirely abandoned in Italy though its use in a basilican church was practically unknown save in the apse. Thus there is a groined vault over the chapel of S. Zeno in S. Prassede, Rome, definitely dated to 817–24, another at SS. Quatro Coronati (847–53), and barrel-vaults at the Calchi palace at Ravenna (eighth century). Two types of masonry were also in use at the same period, then called respectively *opus gallicum* and *opus romanense*, which Kingsley Porter considers were the one rubble and the other brick or brick-laced construction.

The piers of the early Lombard churches, when not retaining the earlier use of columns, were of the simple square or rectangular form, which provided the necessary support for a superstructure of any thickness or strength and formed the first and necessary step towards any attempt to vault the building. The next step was obviously the vaulting of the comparatively narrow span of the side aisles, and to do this the pier assumed a T-form with the leg of the T turned towards the aisle. This form was introduced probably in the tenth century and appears at S. Eustorgio, Milan (recovered by excavation), and rather later at Sta. Sofia, Padua, S. Vittore, Ravenna, and elsewhere. The next step was the adoption of the cruciform pier, from which arches could be sprung in all four directions. One of the earliest known examples of this form was at the church of SS. Felice e Fortunato, Vicenza, dated to the end of the tenth century. S. Carpoforo, Como (1028–40), provides a second example, and the same arrangement, with attached half-columns on each face of the pier, is to be found at S. Miniato al Monte, Florence (1013), and at the early cathedral at Modena (*c.* 1035). It seems probable that at first these responds supported only cross-arches, and though these were soon supplemented by groined vaults over the aisles, it was some time before the same covering was attempted over the main span of the nave. The earlier stage consisted in springing a round arch across the nave between alternate bays and supporting a gabled wall carrying the roof-timbers. This form was (slightly varied) adopted at S. Miniato al Monte, Florence (1013), where the cross-arches appear to be original (Kingsley Porter assigns them to the twelfth century), at S. Carpoforo, Como (consecrated 1040), and a number of other places, and was revived early in the twelfth century at Modena Cathedral, S. Fidele, Como (c. 1115, Kingsley Porter, but possibly of the same date as the church), S. Zeno (Fig. 25), Verona (1138), and elsewhere. At Cremona Cathedral (1129–43) the arches are carried across between each bay. These cross-arches, commonly called diaphragm-arches, were either copied in some of the Norman Romanesque churches of the second half of the eleventh century or less probably were independently evolved in the Norman school.

The adoption of the diaphragm-arch, and subsequently of the vault, over a double bay carried with it the adoption of the alternating system of piers, that is to say, of piers alternately complex to support the cross-arch or vault over the main span, and simple to support only the cross-arch or vault over the aisle. No important church seems to have been built on the uniform system in the second half of the eleventh century, though the system was still employed in some of the smaller churches. The alternate system was still further elaborated after the introduction of the ribbed vault and, in the twelfth-century cathedrals of Cremona, Piacenza, and Parma, seems to have been designed to support sexpartite vaults.

The earliest completely groin-vaulted church in Lombardy, according to Kingsley Porter, is at Mazzone, which he dates to c. 1030. The date has been disputed, but there seems nothing at all improbable in a complete system of groined vaults at this date in Italy when, as we have seen in the previous chapter, the groin-vaulted church makes an earlier appearance in southeastern France. It is, however, with the next step—the introduction of the ribbed vault in Lombardy—that the greatest controversy has arisen. The groined vault is produced by the intersection of two barrel-vaults at right angles to one another, over each bay, and when applied to a wide span has an obvious tendency to sag unless reinforced at its weak points—the groins

—by some system of more stable support such as is supplied
by vaulting-ribs. These ribs, constructed quite independently
of the vault and of dressed stone, formed the necessary system
of arched supports on which the rubble of the actual vault
could rest, and their adoption is the first and most momentous
step in the advance from Romanesque structure towards the
Gothic system. The occasional appearance of ribs in buildings of the Imperial Roman age has little or no bearing on
the subject, as these ribs form an integral part of the vault
itself and have no structural independence. The invention
of the true ribbed vault, then, was made sometime in the
course of the eleventh century, and the two chief competitors
for the honour of priority are Lombardy and the Anglo-
Norman school. The claims of Lombardy have comparatively
recently received considerable re-enforcement from the
researches of Professor Kingsley Porter, who boldly maintained that dated examples are to be found as early as 1040,
and that a continuous series can be produced illustrating the
evolution of this form of vaulting from that date to the twelfth
century. The subject has been complicated by the quite
uncritical statements of other and previous writers who have
claimed even earlier Italian examples, claims which have not
stood the test of criticism and are now generally abandoned.
Thus Rivoira dated the ribbed vaults of Aversa Cathedral to
1049–56, though there is now general agreement that they
date only from the second half of the twelfth century.[1]
Kingsley Porter's own theories have not escaped criticism,
and many of his dates are arrived at by a system of comparative examples and must thus depend only on his theory
of their structural evolution. In spite, however, of certain
reservations M. Camille Enlart[2] was prepared to accept the

[1] Montefiascone was dated by Rivoira to 1032 by a misapplied inscription. It actually dates from c. 1130.
[2] C. Enlart, *Manuel d'archéologie française*, I, Arch. relig., Pt. ii (2nd
ed.), 1920, p. 932.

general conclusion and with it the probability of a Lombard origin for the ribbed vault.

The whole of Kingsley Porter's theory rests ultimately on the date of the building of the church of Sannazzaro, Sessia (near Novara), a structure of the utmost importance, to which he was the first to call attention. There can be little or no doubt that this church was founded about 1040 by Riprando, bishop of Novara, and the surviving ruined western bays retain definite evidence of a ribbed vault of very archaic type. There is thus every probability that here we have a part of the church begun about 1040, but that the surviving portion, which seems to have formed a sort of narthex, was begun or even contemplated in 1040 is open to argument and we should perhaps be safer in assigning a date of some twenty years later to the existing structure, particularly as it formed part of quite a large building, whose construction presumably proceeded from east to west in accordance with the normal medieval practice. The most remarkable part of the vault system at Sannazzaro, Sessia, is that already the Lombard builders had adopted the logical plan of setting the supports of the ribs diagonally across the angle of the bay and facing the direction of the springing of the rib. This idea was not adopted in other Romanesque schools till a far later date.

Kingsley Porter's series is continued by a doubtful example at Lodi Vecchio (aisles), Sannazzaro, Milan (1075–*c.* 1093), S. Anastasia, Asti, Rivolta d'Adda (*c.* 1099), San Michele, Pavia (*c.* 1100, but more probably *c.* 1117) and S. Savino, Piacenza (eastern bays 1107). The system does not appear to have been considered a success, as Lanfranc, the architect of Modena Cathedral, returned in that church to the diaphragm-arch system,[1] and in any case the ribbed vault in Lombardy, however early its appearance, seems to have been more or less stillborn and to have exhibited little or no progressive development. The best known example of the churches of this type

[1] The existing vault is a later addition.

—S. Ambrogio, Milan (Pl. 12*a*, and Fig. 18)—has been omitted from the list cited above as its date has been the subject of more controversy than that of almost any other building in Italy. Kingsley Porter places it in the last half of the eleventh century, but the only direct evidence of its date[1] points definitely to the first third of the twelfth century, perhaps after the great earthquake of 1117. This of course does not apply to the east end, which belonged to the tenth-century church, or to the so-called campanile of the monks.

The typical Lombard vaulting-rib is of simple square section, which is also the only form appearing in the twelfth-century churches of southern Italy.

In the eleventh and twelfth centuries it became usual to cover the crossing of the larger churches with an octagonal dome, similar to that used in Charles the Great's minster at Aachen and copied at San Satiro at Milan in 876. The example at Acqui Cathedral was erected about the middle of the eleventh century and the form becomes frequent in the twelfth century. The barrel-vault also was occasionally used over choirs and transepts.

In plan the later eleventh- and the twelfth-century north Italian churches show considerable variety, for while on the one hand in churches like S. Ambrogio, Milan, the basilican type is retained, in others the transept is markedly developed. This feature becomes general in the early twelfth-century churches of Pavia and received perhaps its most remarkable development in Parma Cathedral, where the arms of the transept have apses at the ends and also on the east side.

---

[1] A document of 1144 relating to a dispute between the canons and the monks asserts that 'the architect of the church had constructed the campanile, as he had constructed the rest of the fabric of the church, out of funds supplied by the city at large'. The campanile (of the canons) had apparently been finished when it was given to the canons by Archbishop Anselm in 1128 and is admittedly a work of that age. See G. Biscaro in *Arch. stor. lomb.*, 1904–5, p. 335, and Baldwin-Brown in *Eng. Hist. Rev.*, xxvi (1911), p. 362.

These with the main east apse form a variety of the trefoiled plan, which was revived in a more elaborate manner and at an earlier date at San Fidele, Como (Fig. 21). Here the transepts have an ambulatory carried completely round them in the same manner as at Sta. Maria im Kapitol, Cologne. The date of the Como church is a little doubtful, but though Porter maintains that it is throughout of the beginning of the twelfth century, its main structure would seem more appropriately placed in the previous century.[1]

Normally the Lombard churches are of two stories only, consisting of the main arcades and the clerestory, but occasionally the latter is replaced by the open tribunes or triforia, as at S. Ambrogio, Milan. The important group of Emilian churches to be considered later is, however, provided with both triforium and clerestory and the same applies to S. Fidele, Como, and a few other churches. The fronts are almost invariably treated with a single low-pitched gable covering the ends of both nave and aisles and having an ascending and descending arcaded gallery below and following the line of the gable. This façade-screen (Pl. 11a) forms one of the most distinctive features of the later Lombard style and differentiates it from most of the other Romanesque schools of Italy. The featuring of this great gabled façade led also to the placing of the western towers, where such existed, touching or free of the western front. Such a pair was planned at S. Giacomo, Como (c. 1105), and exist at Piacenza and Parma Cathedrals, and it seems probable that the scheme was introduced from the north. Twin towers flanking the apse are more typical of Savoy, where they appear early in the eleventh century in the cathedrals of Ivrea and Aosta. S. Abbondio, Como (consecrated 1095), is a notable example in Lombardy. It is

[1] As indicated by the mouldings, the greater part of the north transept is the earliest part of the building (perhaps c. 1000), followed firstly by the crossing and south transept, secondly by the nave, and thirdly by the alterations to the east end.

possible that these towers were a legacy from earlier Carolingian models, but in any case they were also a common feature of German churches of a rather later date.

The normal Lombard campanile was carried up to a considerable height and divided into stages by bands of blind arcading stopped against the shallow clasping buttresses. Sometimes only the belfry stage is pierced by windows, the lower stages being lit only by loops, but more often the three or four upper stages have windows, the number of lights in each window increasing upwards until the maximum of perhaps four lights is reached in the belfry stage; this is very marked in some of the churches at Lucca. Judging from their character the earliest important towers of the Lombard type seem to be those of the cathedral of Ivrea, dating from *c.* 1000; the great campanile of Pomposa Abbey is dated 1063, and others may be mentioned at S. Ambrogio (1128) and S. Satiro, Milan, Sta. Giusta, Susa (eleventh century), and a vast number of other churches.

In addition to the campanili many of the major churches had an octagonal tower or lantern raised above the central crossing. Most of these towers are enriched by an arcaded external gallery and the feature was ultimately developed, as at the Cistercian abbey of Chiaravalle, near Milan, into a lofty many staged erection terminating in a spire.

The blind niches or arcading under the eaves of the early Lombard and first Romanesque churches have been dealt with in the preceding chapter. The feature persisted throughout the period, but late in the eleventh century it received a further development. In the chapel of S. Aquilino, Milan (*c.* 1071), the range of niches communicate with one another and form a covered gallery. This developed into the open arcaded gallery, round the apse, supported on colonnettes, which first appears definitely at S. Giacomo, Como (1095–1117), and in Modena Cathedral (1099–*c* 1120), and from thence onwards on practically all the important churches of the Lombard school. It passed from Italy to Germany, where it was generally adopted in the twelfth century, and into various other countries. The earlier form of niched arcading was considerably elaborated before its final supersession by the arcaded gallery. A good example of this is to be seen in the main apse of S. Pietro, Toscanella (Tuscania), which has a highly ornate treatment consisting of two ranges of blind arcading, two ranges of square-headed niches, and bands of zigzag brick ornament. Much of this church (Pl. 7b, Fig. 19), including the apse, was assigned by Rivoira to the quite incredible date of the first half of the eighth century, solely on the assumption that the Commacine master Rodpertus, who owned property in the town, had something to do with the building. The details, on the other hand, are a definite elaboration of the early Lombard type of ornament and have much in common with rather later work such as that of the campanile at Pomposa safely dated by an inscription to 1063. It seems probable, therefore, that the apse and crossing at Toscanella are of the same date as the crypt, which Rivoira himself assigns to the end of the eleventh century, and the ciborio which is dated 1093.[1]

The doorways of the twelfth-century churches are highly elaborated and provided with numerous recessed orders in the normal Romanesque manner; in addition to this the outer order commonly projects from the face of the wall, forming a shallow porch, and rests upon a free shaft, often set upon the back of a lion or other beast. This feature, which can be met with in Carolingian manuscripts and was ultimately derived from the East, seems first to have been reproduced in stone in southern Italy; the earliest example appears to be that at the cathedral of Acerenza which is perhaps part of

---

[1] There is a definite break in the building between the crossing and the first bay of the nave, though this probably indicates little interval in time. There is a further break between this work and the late twelfth- or early thirteenth-century additions at the west end.

the church begun in 1080. This use of supporting beasts became one of the most noticeable features of the later Italian Romanesque and was transmitted thence to south-eastern France, to the whole of central Europe, and even eventually to Scandinavia and England, though in the last named country the examples are unimportant, few, and late.

The crypt, which forms so prominent a feature of many Italian churches, makes its first appearance, as a single chamber or *confessio* with approaching passages, in the eighth century. It was no doubt imitated from the burial chambers of saints in the suburban catacombs above which a church had subsequently been built. It was gradually enlarged in size until it occasionally extended under the whole church. More commonly, however, it was confined to the eastern part of the building and was set half below and half above the ground-level. The difference in level between the floor of the nave and that of the chancel above the crypt was masked by a wall with open arches called the pontile, with flights of steps ascending to the chancel and descending to the crypt. The crypts themselves are invariably vaulted, commonly with a system of plain groined vaults resting on monolithic columns. Important examples may be mentioned at S. Carpoforo, Como (*c.* 1040), S. Fermo and S. Zeno, Verona, Piacenza Cathedral, and Ancona Cathedral.

The minor details of decoration and ornament of the Lombard churches will best be dealt with separately, but a few words must be said as to the origin of the cubic or cushion-capital which was perhaps first employed by the Lombard builders. Professor Kingsley Porter has been unable to trace it back before the early years of the eleventh century, and cites those at Lomello of *c.* 1025 as the earliest of fully developed type known to him. If so, the cushion-capital makes an equally early appearance in Germany where its use was far more widespread than it ever became in Italy. It seems, however, more probable that it travelled north with so many other Lombard *motifs*, than in the reverse direction, and through Germany reached England before the close of the Anglo-Saxon period.

Emilia. The province of Emilia contains an important group of churches which, while retaining many of the characteristics of the mature Lombard style, is structurally quite distinct, and furthermore exhibits certain minor decorative details which show an influence other than that of the neighbouring province. The churches which form this very distinctive group are the cathedrals of Modena, Parma, Piacenza, and Borgo S. Donnino (Fidenza), all situated on or near the great traffic line represented by the Via Emilia and the modern railway from Ancona to Alessandria. The cathedral of Modena (Fig. 20) was begun in 1099 under a certain Master Lanfranc; in 1106 the altar in the crypt was consecrated by Pascal and in 1184 the whole church was consecrated by Lucius III. At Parma (Pl. 12b, and Fig. 26) the church consecrated in 1106 was destroyed by the great earthquake of 1117. The new church was begun shortly after, only the base of the choir and transept of the earlier structure being retained; it was not finished till early in the thirteenth century. Piacenza Cathedral, begun in 1122, was partly in use in 1158, but was not finished till the thirteenth century. There appears to be no definite evidence of the date of Borgo S. Donnino Cathedral, but its general features indicate a building of the first half of the twelfth century, though here again it seems not to have been finished till the succeeding century.

In plan the churches of the group are very varied, for while Modena retains the simple basilican form with three apses, Parma and Piacenza both display varieties of the fully developed cruciform plan in which the arms of the transepts terminate in apses, a local variety of the trilobed plan, which is also to be seen in the cathedral of S. Ciriaco, Ancona (Marches). Parma and Borgo S. Donnino were both designed with a pair of towers flanking the west front. It is, however, in the internal elevation that these Emilian churches differ most markedly from those of Lombardy. In each case they exhibit the three-storied structure (main arcade, triforium, and clerestory) which is definitely to be derived from north of the Alps and is only prominent elsewhere in Italy in the Apulian churches of the Bari group, the type church of S. Nicola being slightly earlier in date. In each case the Emilian churches have the alternating simple and compound pier producing a double bay, but though all have ribbed vaults only the church of Borgo S. Donnino seems to have received the vault for which it was designed. This is a quadripartite vault over the double bay, with no wall-shaft running up from the intermediate pier, but with the clerestory windows spaced together in evident reference to the vault as it exists. Modena was not originally intended to receive a vault at all, provision being made only for the great cross-arches which divide its double bays. Parma was apparently designed for a sexpartite vault, similar to that erected in the thirteenth century over the nave of Piacenza, but actually received a quadripartite vault over each bay.[1]

The presence of figures from the Arthurian romance-cycle (Arthur himself, Gawain, Kay the seneschal, and others), among the sculptured decorations of the cathedral of Modena and of a figure from the legend of Alexander on the church of Borgo S. Donnino has been held by M. Mâle to indicate the presence of French *jongleurs* on the main pilgrim route to Rome, Monte Gargano, and Brindisi for Jerusalem. The pilgrimage to Monte S. Angelo on Monte Gargano particularly appealed to the Norman French from association with their own Mont St. Michel, and the prominence of the Arthurian cycle perhaps indicates a northern rather than a

---

[1] The minor churches of Piacenza seem to indicate the development of vaulting in this province. Sta. Eufemia, dating probably from the second half of the eleventh century, has a groined vault over the double bay, while S. Savino, consecrated in 1107, has a ribbed vault over the double bay.

southern French influence. However this may be, this group of churches, particularly Borgo S. Donnino, presents closer affinities, in its internal ordinance, with Norman Romanesque than with any other northern school.

In external appearance, on the other hand, the Emilian churches are purely Lombard, retaining the single gabled façade of that province and the arcaded galleries to apse, pediment, and side walls.

Venice. The art and architecture of eleventh- and twelfth-century Venice are so overpoweringly Byzantine that little need be said on the subject. The city and its territory, however, produced a local type of campanile of which the general lines were perhaps settled by the great tower of S. Marco which is said to have been begun in the tenth century. The arcaded belfry was a work of the sixteenth century and the whole structure collapsed in 1902. Since this catastrophe the finest ancient Venetian campanile is that at Torcello, and there are others of the same type at Murano, S. Martino, Chioggia, and elsewhere in the Islands. The tower at Torcello is carried up without a break and windowless from the ground to the belfry, the surfaces being only relieved by shallow buttresses finished with Lombard arcading at the top. The actual belfry has four open arches in each face.

The church at Murano, reconstructed in the first half of the twelfth century, is unusual as being of pronounced cruciform plan entirely without crossing-arches, and also as having an elaborate Lombard gallery round the east end. This church together with S. Fosca, Torcello, provide examples of the deep zigzag frieze which seems to be a local peculiarity.

Tuscany. Apart from Lombardy the most important province of northern Italy, so far as Romanesque architecture is concerned, is Tuscany. This province, however, is sharply divided within itself into two main schools centred in the city-states of Pisa and Florence. Pisa owes some of its character to Lombardy, but developed its own local school of

Romanesque, a subsidiary school at Lucca produced a blend of Lombard and Pisan, while Florence held fast to classical traditions and may be hardly said to have produced Romanesque at all.

The character of Pisan Romanesque was settled once and for all by the building of the cathedral, which marked the maritime supremacy of the republic and in particular the action at Palermo in 1062. The cathedral was founded in 1063, a certain Buschetto, whose sarcophagus and epitaph survive, being the master-of-the-works. A consecration took place in 1118 when the church was far from finished, the façade indeed not being completed until the thirteenth century. Although considerably altered and restored the building provides an admirable example of nearly all the features which distinguish Pisan Romanesque. It is of course built on a vast scale and has deeply projecting transepts and a nave with double aisles. Unlike most of the other churches of the district it is a three-storied building, the triforium having a main arch enclosing sub-arches. The main apse has an external arcaded gallery of the Lombard type. The distinctive features of Pisan Romanesque are firstly the free use of marble casing generally banded in a second colour and the enrichment of the external wall-surface by a tall continuous wall-arcade standing on a fairly high plinth. This type of arcading was certainly used at an earlier date in several Armenian churches such as the cathedral (989–1001) and St. Gregory (1001) at Ani and at Marmaschen (988–1029), and Enlart suggests the possibility that Pisan trade with the East may to some extent explain its transmission to Europe. Whether this be so or not this arcading was almost universal in the Pisan churches and was copied in the subsidiary schools of Lucca, Pistoia, Sardinia, and Troia. Normally under the head of each arch is a recessed lozenge-shaped panel, sometimes exchanged for the round form, and enclosing a marble mosaic or other enrichment.

Even more distinctive of the Pisan style is the treatment of the façade which, in contrast to the single gabled screen of the Lombard churches, follows the outline of the building itself in having a high central gable and raking walls at the ends of the aisles. The whole available space is covered by a series of open arcaded galleries, set one above the other and running horizontally across the building, again in contrast with the single ascending and descending gallery of the Lombard school. This treatment produces an effect of great richness, which is enhanced, on the cathedral at Pisa, by the free use of marble mosaic in the spandrels.

The Pisan churches show their further independence of the Lombard school by the almost entire absence of any attempt at stone-vaulting. The cathedral, as built, was roofed throughout in timber and the minor churches followed the same lead. As a result there is a much freer use of the simple column as a support than farther north, there being no high strain on the superstructure.

Two other buildings of the same period form part of the cathedral group at Pisa—the cylindrical Leaning Tower, begun in 1174 and finished c. 1350, and the baptistery, of which the lower part only is Romanesque (begun 1153). Both of these structures show the distinctive Pisan arcading, and the Leaning Tower is remarkable for the attempts of each succeeding architect to rectify, in part, the tilt of the lower stages. The minor churches of the town display the same decorative features as the cathedral. Among them may be noted S. Paolo a ripa d'Arno (Fig. 27) as the church presenting the closest analogy with the cathedral of Troia in Apulia, the chief example of the Pisan type in that part of the country.

The splendid group of churches at Lucca (Pl. 13a) follows closely the Pisan model except for the campanili, which are of purely Lombard form. It will be sufficient to mention the cathedral (façade begun 1204), S. Frediano (1112–47), S. Michele (twelfth century), and Sta. Maria Forisportam. At

Pistoia is a minor group which includes the cathedral (mainly thirteenth century) and the ornate but very monotonous flank of San Giovanni fuor Civitas (end of the twelfth century). Scattered over Tuscany are other examples such as Sta. Maria della Pieve, Arezzo, and the cathedral of Massa Marittima. The island of Sardinia was also under Pisan architectural influence and many of the churches here, such as Borutta, Codrongianus, and the cathedral of Portotorres, have distinctive Pisan features.

The most unexpected product of the Pisan school, however, is to be found in Apulia, where, as we have said, Troia Cathedral is almost a replica of a Pisan church. Miss E. Jackson has shown,[1] historically, how such influence might well have been brought to bear in the eleventh and twelfth centuries, and indeed there can be no doubt of a direct artistic connexion between the two. Troia Cathedral (Pl. 13b) was built between c. 1093 and 1127 and the series is carried on by features in the tomb of Bohemund at Canosa (early twelfth century), Siponto Cathedral (early twelfth century, restored later), Foggia (begun 1179) and others. In some of these buildings the Pisan features are found in conjunction with a totally different structural system of local or Byzantine character.

The Florentine equivalent of Romanesque is distinguished by a very close adherence to classical forms, an extreme simplicity of structural decoration, and by the free use of a veneer of marble forming polychrome bands and panelling. Only two buildings are of first importance, S. Miniato al Monte (Pl. 11b, and Fig. 22) and the baptistery. The first of these was begun in 1013 and finished towards the end of the century, but was altered in the twelfth century. As in the Pisan school, there is no attempt to make use of stone vaulting. S. Miniato, however, has a series of diaphragm-arches set unusually

---

[1] E. Jackson, 'Pisan churches on the Via Traiana', in *Brit. Arch. Ass. Journ.*, N.S., XXXV, p. 163.

between each three bays. All the details are strongly classical,
the intermediate supports are columns, and the whole structure
depends for its effect on its marble casing. The same remarks
apply to the baptistery (late eleventh century), where the
internal elevation is of the purest Corinthian form with
fluted pilasters and horizontal entablatures. Identical general
features are to be found in the fronts of the Badia at Fiesole
(end of the eleventh century) and at S. Andrea, Empoli (dated
1093).

Set in the heart of Tuscany is the remarkable abbey-church
of S. Antimo,[1] begun about 1118, which for some unexplained
reason presents the purely French plan of an ambulatory and
three radiating apsidal chapels. The high roofs, however, are
of timber and the groined vaulting is confined to the aisles.
As usual, the pilgrim route has been called in to explain this
anomaly, but some more definite solution seems to be required
to account for the single example of a French church of this age
between the frontier and southern Italy.

A single feature of two Umbrian churches perhaps deserves
a passing mention. The west front of the cathedral at Assisi
is ornamented by a curious panelling or grille of horizontal
and vertical mouldings which is more curious than attractive.
A somewhat similar treatment may also be seen on the façade
of S. Pietro, Spoleto, and, curiously enough, on the front of
the church of S. Giusta, near Bazzano, in the Abruzzi.

Rome. The classical traditions of Rome were of so strong
and enduring a nature that they resisted in turn the Byzantine,
Romanesque, and Gothic styles and survived but little altered
to be swallowed up in the Renaissance. There is consequently
little genuine Romanesque to be found in Rome itself or in
its immediate neighbourhood. A single Roman church, SS.
Giovanni e Paolo, is partly a structure in the Lombard style
of the early part of the twelfth century, with the typical
arcaded gallery round the apse. Otherwise the churches of

[1] C. Enlart in *Rev. de l'art chrétien*, lxiii (1912), 1.

the period are architecturally indistinguishable from those of the earlier ages.[1] The attitude of the twelfth-century Romans in these matters may be judged from the oft quoted inscription on the patchwork tower of Niccolo Crescenzio, built of classical fragments, 'not from motives of ambition but to revive the ancient glories of Rome'. A feature which may, however, be fairly classed as Romanesque and which is still amongst the most prominent in almost any view of the city, is the fine series of brick campanili which were added to many of the churches during this period. In spite of much controversy in the past there can be no doubt that these towers were almost all erected during the eleventh, twelfth, and thirteenth centuries. They consist, generally, of a blind base-story about equal in height to the roof of the adjoining church and are divided above this point into stages by horizontal cornices of classical type. These stages vary in number up to seven and are lit by openings of two or more lights with round arches and dividing shafts set centrally in the wall. The surviving campanili number some thirty-six and the type is hardly to be found outside Rome and the immediate neighbourhood. Perhaps the best preserved examples are those of S. Alessio, Sta. Cecilia, SS. Giovanni e Paolo, Sta. Maria in Cosmedin, Sta. Maria in Trastevere, and S. Silvestro in Capite,[2] in Rome, and the cathedrals of Sermoneta and Tivoli.

The only other type of Roman structure with any claims to be considered Romanesque is the series of cloisters, such as those at St. John Lateran and St. Paul without the Walls. These, however, belong to the larger study of the Roman marble-workers, which hardly comes within the scope of the present work.

South Italy. As M. Bertaux has justly observed, through-

[1] San Prassede, it may be noted, however, received a re-enforcement of diaphragm-arches in the twelfth century.
[2] *Journ. R.I.B.A.*, 3rd ser., v, p. 213. The dating here given is quite mistaken.

out the Middle Ages Italy was artistically divided into the north and south by the almost impassable barrier afforded by the papal state on the west and the mountain *massif* of the Abruzzi on the east. As we have seen, Rome proved almost impermeable to the Romanesque and she was equally in-different in turn to the Gothic style. Century after century she reproduced the ancient forms of church architecture with little or no variation until they were adopted, revivified, and transformed by the architects of the Renaissance. The Abruzzi filled the gap between the papal state and the Adriatic and, though traversed by the pilgrim route to Monte Gargano, their isolated valley population, largely cut off from the outside world and from one another formed an artistic backwater which was almost as impenetrable as the con-servatism of Rome.

The two chief forces of Italian Romanesque, the Lombard and Pisan on the north and the Norman Apulian and the Norman Sicilian on the south, extended up to this barrier on either side and in places penetrated it, but in only one group do we find definite traces of north Italian building in the south, and the traces of southern art in the north are still more fugitive.

The Romanesque architecture of southern Italy is centred in two districts, from which it spread only partially and at a late date over the rest of the country. The first of these is the province of Apulia which produced a flourishing school centred at Bari, the later capital of the duchy. The second is the Norman kingdom of Sicily, centred at the capital Palermo, which produced a hybrid architecture which ex-tended, in the thirteenth or late in the previous century, into the province of Campania where its late flowering is almost the only expression of Romanesque art which that province affords.

It should be borne in mind that before the arrival of the Normans the south of Italy was divided between the Eastern

Emperors who held Apulia, Calabria, and the Basilicata; the independent duchies of Naples, Sorrento, Amalfi, and Benevento; and the Saracen emirate of Sicily. Naples and the neighbouring states represented the native tradition, which, Greek in ultimate origin, was Italian by adoption and was still further influenced by a shadowy Byzantine overlordship; Benevento, though long the centre of Lombard power in the south, shows little trace of northern art; Byzantine art was all powerful in the provinces still directly appertaining to the Eastern Empire; while Sicily was divided between the same influence and the vigorous Islamic art which was the product of Sassanian or Byzantine originals or a blend of both.

It is to this queer mosaic of races and of political and artistic influences that the Norman conquest brought yet another element further to involve the pattern and to render the segregation of its component parts still more intricate and involved.

It is fortunately only necessary for the purpose we have in view to endeavour to disentangle the influence brought to bear on the local art by the Normans themselves, for it is only after the Norman conquest, and probably as a direct result, that anything that can be termed Romanesque made its appearance in southern Italy. As a preface to this inquiry it will be well to recall the salient features of that conquest before turning our attention to its architectural effects in the two chief centres of Norman rule.

The prolific Hauteville family sprang from the castle of Hauteville-le-Guichard some eight miles north of Coutances in Normandy. Nearly all of the sons of Tancred de Hauteville by his two wives sought their fortunes in Italy. Between 1030 and 1043 three of the elder family appear in southern Italy at the head of the bands of Norman soldiery which had already arrived in the country. In 1041 they became possessed of Melfi and in three battles defeated the forces of the Greek 'Catapan' sent against them, thus gaining possession

of most of Apulia. Robert Guiscard, a brother of the second
family, arrived in Italy in 1053, and within the next few years
came four more brothers, including the youngest, Roger, the
future ruler of Sicily. By force of arms and by deceit they
made themselves masters of both Apulia and Calabria, and
in 1059 Robert was created Duke by the Pope, calling himself Duke of Apulia and Calabria and future Duke of Sicily
'if the grace of God and St. Peter help me'. In 1061 Robert
Guiscard and Roger landed at Messina, called in by the rebel
ibn Thimna, and in 1072 the fall of Palermo broke the
Saracen power, though the conquest of Sicily was not complete till 1091. The lordship of the island passed to Roger,
Robert Guiscard returning to the mainland after the fall of
Palermo. Here Bari had been taken in 1071 and Salerno was
taken in 1076. Robert Guiscard died in 1085 and was buried
with others of his house in the abbey of Venosa, near Melfi.
Roger I, Count of Sicily, was succeeded by his son, Roger II,
who obtained the title of king in 1130. Under him were
united the Norman possessions on the mainland. Naples
came finally under Norman rule in 1137. The Norman
dynasty, in the persons of the two Rogers, William I (1154–
66), and William II (1166–89), lasted over a century and
their traditions were to a certain extent carried on by their
successors the Swabian princes, particularly the Emperor
Frederick II.

It is a curious fact that throughout the first generation of
Norman rule there is practically no trace of northern influence in the art and architecture of either Apulia or Sicily.
The first church of the abbey of Venosa, consecrated in 1059
and built as the burial place of the house of Hauteville, has
nothing to recall its northern founders, and the same may
be said of other buildings of southern Italy built or restored
under the direct influence of the early Norman princes. It
was only towards the end of the eleventh century that the
Apulian Romanesque makes its appearance at Bari and it is

not until well on in the reign of Roger II that any symptoms
of Romanesque can be discerned in Sicily. These two schools
must now engage our attention.

Apulian Romanesque. The prototype of Apulian Romanesque architecture is the Benedictine Abbey church of S.
Nicola at Bari (Pl. 14*a*, and Fig. 23), built to house the relics
of St. Nicholas of Myra brought here in 1087. The church
was in course of construction in 1089 and the crypt was built
by 1090. A synod was held in the upper church in 1098, when
the still existing throne was made. The church appears to have
been well advanced at the death of Abbot Elia (in 1105), who
is credited with its construction. It was, however, not actually
finished in 1132 and a consecration took place in 1197. S.
Nicola is a large aisled church with a transept, three apses projecting to the east, and two towers flanking the west front. The
original building is remarkable for its height and economy
of external ornament, which is confined to shallow surface
arcading and recalls the forms of northern Romanesque only
in its general lines. It is, however, the internal structure
which seems a definite importation from the north, for the
great nave is divided into arcade, triforium, and clerestory of
normal northern proportions and is only paralleled in Italy
in the group of churches of Emilia. The triforium, with three
sub-arches under a main outer order, in each bay, opens on
to a passage above the groined vaults of the aisles, and the
clerestory has a single round-headed window in each bay.
So far the ordinance is definitely northern, but the main
arcades rest on monolithic columns in the classical tradition
and there is no attempt to carry up wall-shafts between the
bays in the Norman manner except above the single compound pier on each side which divides the nave into two
parts. The aisles have heavy buttresses with arches between
forming a series of tall arched bays or recesses. The nave
itself has a timber roof. It will be seen that the general
arrangement is northern and, generally speaking, non-Italian,

but that it is derived from a Norman original, as Bertaux suggests, is by no means so certain. It is true that the triforium and the general proportions of the building are similar to those at Jumièges (begun c. 1040) and that the use of monolithic piers renders the employment of wall-shafts difficult, but there is no attempt at the double bay and the alternating pier which is so marked a feature of the Norman church. The two towers, furthermore, that flank the western front are set beyond the aisles in a fashion unknown in Normandy but which may perhaps be inspired by the towers at S. Ambrogio at Milan and elsewhere in northern Italy. We may on the whole accept Professor Kingsley Porter's[1] conclusion that S. Nicola at Bari is the combined result of local, Lombard, and Norman influences, but it is the northern or Norman contribution which gives to it and its imitators the remarkable characteristics of the Apulian school. It would seem likely that the building of S. Nicola had a direct influence on the design of the three-storied cathedral of Modena begun in 1099, and which, in its way, is as isolated in north Italy as S. Nicola is in the south. Many details both of design and decoration point in this direction, though each building has distinctive features which are entirely foreign to the other.

In Apulia S. Nicola almost at once became the model for a whole series of churches, the first of which is the imposing cathedral of Trani which stands upon a complete subterranean church.[2] Begun in 1098 and continued well into the twelfth century, the cathedral no doubt owes its importance to the fame of a local saint, S. Nicola Pelegrino. In plan it resembles the Bari church and has a developed triforium and

---

[1] 'Compostella, Bari and Romanesque Architecture'. A. K. Porter in *Art Studies* (Harvard and Princeton), 1923, p. 7.

[2] The crypt under the nave is said to be the earlier church. This theory is quite untenable as in materials, design, and decoration the whole of the crypt appears to be of the same age as the superstructure. This, of course, does not apply to the early confessio below the main crypt.

the same series of arches between the main buttresses of the aisles.

With the exception of the church of S. Nicola, all the churches of Bari were destroyed by William II (the Bad) of Sicily when he took the city in 1156. This led to the entire rebuilding of the cathedral in the second half of the twelfth century. The new church was of the same general plan as S. Nicola with all those features which were distinctive of the Apulian school. The most remarkable of these was the enclosing of the whole of the east end, with its apse, by a lofty buttressed wall of rectangular plan and having two campanili within the two east angles. Another feature was the placing of a light and graceful open gallery or arcade (Pl. 14*b*) as a crown to the series of blind arches between the aisle buttresses. The cathedral also received an octagonal central cupola with an extremely rich external decoration. This eastern screen-wall, which appears only in the Apulian school and must thus have been evolved within it, was present in the original design of the Church of S. Nicola, though Bertaux maintains it to be an addition.[1] Here also existed the external gallery over the aisle, for while the north gallery is an addition, the south gallery forms an integral part of the original structure. The eastern screen with the two towers was repeated in the cathedrals of Bitonto (begun 1175), Giovinazzo (late twelfth century), and Molfetta (late twelfth century). In the last instance, however, it is found in conjunction with a domed church of quite different character. The collegiate church of Barletta (probably begun in 1139) is worthy of mention as one of the S. Nicola group, having the groined vaults of the aisles raised above the triforium level, though it is more than doubtful if this be the original arrangement.

Side by side with these distinctively Romanesque churches

[1] The spacing of the original blind-arcading of the external walls and its continuity affords ample proof that the transept and eastern screen are of one build.

Apulia produced at the same period a series of domed churches in the Byzantine tradition which are remarkable for the local system of supporting the domes of the main span by half-vaults over the aisles.[1]

Yet another element in the architecture of the province is the rather surprising appearance there of a series of churches which by their structure or decoration or both proclaim their close affinity with the Pisan Lombardic style. These have already been dealt with under that heading.

Finally attention must be called to a small group of south Italian churches which adopted the purely French type of plan of the apse, ambulatory, and radiating chapels. There can be no manner of doubt of the French origin of this plan, which occurs in three instances only in the south and once again in Tuscany in the course of the twelfth century. The most important of these churches is the unfinished second church of the abbey of Venosa, probably begun before 1135. Even in its ruined and unfinished state it is one of the most imposing Romanesque monuments of south Italy. The neighbouring cathedral of Acerenza was probably a direct copy of the church at Venosa. Both display the external Lombard bands and arcading. The third church is the cathedral of Aversa, near Naples, which Rivoira tried to place in the middle of the eleventh century. It is not exactly dated, but it is obvious that a church of French type can hardly have been erected in south Italy before the type (in this particular form) was current in France. Bertaux ascribes it to the middle or second half of the twelfth century, which brings it into line with the other Italian churches of the same type. It is remarkable as possessing ribbed vaulting, which is extremely uncommon in the south till the thirteenth century. The earliest dated example appears to be in the remains of Teramo Cathedral, built immediately before or after 1156.

---

[1] e.g. Canosa Cathedral, Ognissanti, Valenzano, Molfetta Cathedral, &c.

All these twelfth-century ribbed vaults have plain square ribs
like the early vaulting-ribs of Lombardy.

Sicilian Romanesque. We have seen that Sicily before the
Norman conquest was more than half Moslem and the rest
Greek. After the conquest Latin sees were created and given
to Frenchmen from Normandy, Brittany, Provence, and
Savoy. The new rulers, however, made a policy of protect-
ing all creeds alike; Roger I himself built Greek churches
in Palermo, and if he did not actually build mosques he
allowed them to be built. This policy was continued by his
successors, and as a result the twelfth-century architecture
of Sicily is partly Moslem, partly Greek, and partly Romanesque. The actual court of Palermo leaned heavily towards
the Moslem element and the pleasure-houses and palaces
of the Favara, Menani (Roger II), la Ziza (William I) and
la Cuba (William II) were almost purely Moslem both in
form and decoration. So also is the decoration of the nave
of the Capella Palatina at Palermo (1129–43), though the
plan of the building is Latin and the structure partly Greek.
The church of the Martorana (1143), built for the Greek rite
by the Admiral George of Antioch, was, in its original state,
a purely Greek church, and the domed churches of S. Giovanni degli Eremiti (founded 1148) and S. Cataldo (1161) are
partly Greek and partly Moslem, the domes resting on that
peculiarly awkward form of squinch-arch in recessed orders
which oversail the wall-surface, which is characteristic of the
contemporary dome-construction of Cairo.

It is chiefly in the great cathedrals that Romanesque forms
make a tardy appearance. Cefalu Cathedral was begun
in 1131, Messina Cathedral (destroyed by earthquake 1908)
was restored by Roger II but not consecrated till 1207,
Palermo Cathedral was completed and dedicated in 1185, and
the Cathedral of Monreale, the greatest achievement of the
Norman rule, was built by William II between 1174 and
1182. The plans of all these churches are Romanesque, with

three eastern apses, forming a deeply projecting presbytery
and side chapels, transept, and an aisled nave. Cefalu, Monreale, and Troina have towers flanking the west front which
are, however, set partly beyond the aisles, and probably all
had an open narthex set between the towers such as still exists
at Cefalu. There is, however, no attempt at a triforium story,
the space between the main arcades and the clerestory being
devoted to or at least intended for mosaic decoration. An unusual local type of plan is provided by the Chiese dei Vespri,
Palermo (*temp*. William II), and La Badiazza, near Messina.[1]
In both these churches there is a half-hearted attempt to
produce a transept with east and west aisles though the arms
project only one bay from the crossing and barely beyond
the nave aisles. The interiors of these Sicilian churches
universally display the pointed arch, commonly stilted in the
Moslem manner and resting on cylindrical columns.

Of all the Sicilian churches the cathedral of Cefalu[2] (Pl.
15*a*, and Fig. 24) is the most Romanesque in its external
characteristics. Its surfaces are covered with a profusion of
intersecting wall-arcades and the lofty general proportions
are quite foreign to Italy. The presbytery, south transept,
and nave-aisles received a system of ribbed vaulting, but
this, according to Arata, is a subsequent addition. The free
use of intersecting arcades is common to many Sicilian
churches, as Palermo and Monreale (Pl. 15*b*) Cathedrals and
the Vespri at Palermo. As it does not appear before the second
quarter of the twelfth century it may reasonably be derived
from Norman originals, in which school it makes its appearance round about the year 1100. Bertaux, it is true, considered it to be of Moslem origin, but the examples he

---

[1] This church, endowed by William II and now much ruined, is
remarkable as having possessed a complete series of ribbed vaults, except
for a dome over the crossing.

[2] The west front was built or rebuilt, according to an inscription, in
1240, and the nave roof lowered and rebuilt in 1263. See 'Notes on the
Cathedral Church of Cefalu, Sicily'. G. Hubbard, *Arch*. lvi. 57.

cites[1] are unconvincing, and it seems more reasonable to ascribe it to the influence of the Normans, more especially as they certainly introduced their characteristic chevron-ornament into Sicily. This last appears in each of the three great cathedrals we are dealing with and survived in Sicily through the thirteenth and even into the fourteenth century. It makes also a sporadic appearance at Melfi and the district of the Vulture, the early centre of Norman power, and curiously enough in a few churches of northern Italy.[2] A third distinctive ornament of Sicilian Romanesque is the cushion or gadrooned voussoir, which appears also in the crusading monuments of Palestine and very occasionally in France. The earliest dated example of the feature, however, appears to be in the Bab el Futtuh, Cairo, erected in 1087, and the origin must thus be Islamic.

The cathedral of Palermo has been greatly altered, but is remarkable for its crypt, which lies immediately east of the main structure, a pair of eastern towers, and a curious juxtaposition of Norman and Islamic ornament. Monreale Cathedral, save for its plan, shows a return to pre-Norman traditions; its proportions are somewhat squat and its roofs are of timber. The arches throughout are pointed, but are not so stilted as the earlier examples. Its most Romanesque feature is the incomparable cloister which displays the sculpture of the age in its most accomplished form.

The art of Norman Sicily is one of the most brilliant and intriguing episodes in the history of medieval culture, but it must be admitted that it owes all or nearly all its most attractive features to the earlier cultures which it supplanted. Its mosaics are purely Byzantine, its honeycombed and painted roofs are equally purely Islamic. The pointed arches

[1] An Islamic example, dated to 980, is, however, to be found at the Cristo de la Luz, Toledo.
[2] Sta. Maria Maggiore, Toscanella, and S. Pancrazio, Corneto, in the Roman province, S. Clemente in Casauria in the Abruzzi, and farther north at Genoa Cathedral and Montechiaro d'Asti (Alessandria).

of its buildings are due to the same source and it is only in the monumental length and scale of the major buildings and in certain features of their plan that the influence of the north becomes apparent. The stone-sculpture of the cloisters belongs to the common stock of southern Romanesque and the distinctively Norman features are confined to the two decorative motives we have described above.

It is, however, one of these motives, the interlacing arcade, that, developed and orientalized in Sicily, was introduced thence in the thirteenth century into the southern part of the conservative province of Campania. Here in the cities of Amalfi, Ravello, and Salerno, the art of Sicily produced that bizarre group of buildings which remind one of the florid splendours of late Islamic art. Three cloisters (*c.* 1250) and the cathedral campanile (1276) at Amalfi, the cloister of S. Domenico, Salerno, the Palazzo Rufolo (*c.* 1280) at Ravello, and the campanile at Gaeta (1279) are the prominent examples of this style.

The two campanili either are or were finished with five cupolas and are obvious imitations of the tower of the Martorana at Palermo. The cloisters have an elaborate system of intersecting pointed arches which in effect resemble the plain intersecting window-tracery of the fourteenth century in this country. The same decoration is carried to extremes in the Rufola palace, which, it must be admitted, is more than reminiscent of a kiosk at some modern exhibition.

Centrally Planned Churches. Every period of European architecture has produced a certain number of buildings designed on what is generally termed the central plan. These buildings all possess the essential feature that their four quarters are more or less symmetrical; their form, however, may vary from the simple square or round to the most elaborate combinations of the cruciform and apsidal plan. They form a class distinct from the general mass of church-building and as such will be more conveniently treated separately under each individual country.

Most of the centrally planned buildings of the Romanesque period in Italy followed one or other of the types belonging to a preceding age. Like their predecessors they belong to three classes—the church proper, the baptistery, and the sepulchral chapel. The churches of this type are commonly round, following the type set by S. Stefano Rotundo, Rome, S. Angelo, Perugia, and Sta. Sofia, Benevento. The first dates probably from the fourth century, the second from the sixth, while Sta. Sofia was founded in the seventh. The Roman and Beneventan churches have double arcades, while the church of S. Angelo is a building with an internal colonnade of sixteen bays and formerly possessed four chapels projecting towards the cardinal points. The roofs of all these churches are of timber. The old cathedral at Brescia is of similar type but of later date and has groined vaults to the aisle. Other examples may be noted at Sta. Maria Madalina, Nocera, S. Tomaso in Limine (near Bergamo), and S. Pietro, Asti. The last is perhaps due to the Knights of St. John of Jerusalem who were established here in 1182, though the church is generally assigned to an earlier date. Of churches directly inspired by the Holy Sepulchre at Jerusalem S. Giovanni al Sepolcro at Brindisi is indicated by its dedication, but the most remarkable structure of this class is S. Stefano, Bologna, with its attendant complex of buildings. There seems no particular reason to doubt the early tradition that S. Petronio, in the fifth century, in veneration of the Holy Places, built close to the church of SS. Vitale and Agricola a group of buildings in imitation of the churches of Constantine at Jerusalem. In any case the Lombard king Liutprant gave the marble basin called the 'basin of Pilate' which still stands in the atrium. The whole group of buildings was largely or entirely reconstructed late in the eleventh or early in the twelfth century, but still reflects a general idea of the former arrangement of the Holy Places before their reconstruction by the Crusaders. The church representing

that of the Holy Sepulchre itself is an irregular polygon with
an arcade of twelve bays. The external wall with its ornamental banding and diapering has an appearance of greater
age than the twelfth century, and may in fact be an earlier
survival.

The remarkable Justinian church of S. Vitale, Ravenna,
not only inspired the builders of Charlemagne's minster at
Aachen but seems to have aroused an equal and more tutored
admiration in Italy itself. Theobald, bishop of Arezzo,
provided funds in 1026 for the architect Maginardo to travel
to Ravenna to study the monuments there. As a result he
built the old cathedral at Arezzo on the model of S. Vitale;
it was unfortunately destroyed by Cosimo de Medici in
1561. Another earlier type to be copied at the same period
was that of the Carolingian churches of Germigny-des-
Prés and S. Satiro, Milan, an eastern model derived perhaps
from Armenia and consisting of a square body with four
piers supporting the roof and as many apses projecting from
the side walls. This was no doubt the basis of the plan
of the remarkable church of S. Claudio at Chienti, built
probably early in the eleventh century. It has a pair of
cylindrical towers flanking the west front and certainly of
Carolingian descent. Another church of somewhat similar
character is Sta. Maria del Tiglio, Gravedona.

The second class of building to which the central type of
plan is particularly applicable is the baptistery, and in this
direction the Italian architects had an opportunity that was
largely lacking in other countries. Elsewhere in western
Europe the building of large separate baptisteries had become obsolete at a much earlier date, but in Italy the
practice remained in full force throughout the Romanesque
period. Many of these structures, such as that at Arsago,
followed the much earlier plan of an octagon with alternate
square and semicircular niches in the internal walls, to be
seen at Fréjus, Novara, and elsewhere. The great bap-

tisteries of the age, however, though based on the same plan,
are of vast dimensions and imposing height. Such are the
late eleventh-century building at Florence and those at
Cremona (1167) and Parma (1196). The baptistery at Pisa
is on an even more imposing scale and is a circular structure
with an internal arcade.

The third class of building—the sepulchral chapel—is
perhaps only represented, in our period, by a single building, the tomb of the crusader Bohemund, prince of Antioch
(*d.* 1111), at Canosa. In all its essential features, and in some
of its decoration, this is the tomb-house of a Moslem prince,
and is surmounted by the 'kubbet' or dome which in early
Islamic art always marks a holy place or tomb.

Ornament and Sculpture. Comparatively little use is made
in Italian Romanesque of those purely geometrical enrichments of the orders of the arches which are the main feature
of English twelfth-century ornament. We have already
touched upon the occasional use of such imported forms as
the chevron-ornament from the north and the gadrooned
or cushion-voussoir from the south; apart from these the
only similar enrichment in common use is the cable-orna-
ment cut on the surface of a roll-moulding. Of much less
frequent occurrence is the Carolingian pelta-ornament, used
as a diaper on roll-mouldings at Piacenza, Modena, Cremona,
and Ferrara Cathedrals. The Greek fret also makes an occasional appearance. Commonly the recessed orders of a door-
head are either simply moulded or left square and carved on
the surface with running enrichment. This enrichment is
nearly always one form or another of acanthus-scroll with or
without birds, beasts, or human figures disposed within it.
The acanthus-scroll, at any rate in the north, commonly has
a stem composed of three strands, a trick of the carver which
was probably inherited from the universal use of the triple
strand interlace in Italy at an earlier date. In the north the
acanthus is commonly of the Roman type and occasionally

develops into those full and florid scrolls distinctive of the late imperial age and which were revived in Pisa and occasionally elsewhere. To the same type belong the stiff and somewhat gross acanthus-rosettes which were not uncommonly used in the panels of pulpits. When this Roman type of acanthus, with birds and beasts, appears in southern Italy it is commonly to be ascribed to a northern influence, as owing to the basic Byzantine character of south Italian art the native form in that part of the country was the spiny acanthus of Byzantine tradition. This form is used profusely in southern decoration both in its scrolled form and as individual leaves set radially round an arch or label to form a continuous enrichment. The derivative form of so-called fennel-leaf decoration, more appropriate to a meagre type of ornament, is diffused throughout Italy in the early Romanesque period and continues to make an occasional appearance, till the thirteenth century, in confined spaces where a more florid form would be inappropriate.

In some of the Pavian churches an acanthus decoration is to be met with, consisting of a regular diaper or brocade pattern of palmette leaves, carved on the surface of a shaft or the face of an order; the same detail may be found in a few other churches, such as Genoa Cathedral. Apart from the acanthus the only other foliage at all of frequent occurrence is the vine-scroll, and this is more usual in the thirteenth than in the twelfth century.

The use of carved bands of ornament to relieve a plain wall-surface is not unusual in the middle period of the Lombard school. The early twelfth-century churches of Pavia are thus enriched with bands of carving of which the staple *motif* is the grotesque beast or monster rendered in a barbaric style. Bands of figure-carving appear on the front of Modena Cathedral, but normally in this part of the country the carved panels are massed symmetrically to the right and left of the doorway. A rich running frieze, based on the acanthus, is carried round the exterior of the central cupola of Bari Cathedral.

We have already referred to the well-known Italian practice of setting the flanking columns of the main doorways on the backs of lions or some other beasts. This, according to Mâle, was the revival of an ancient eastern *motif* which had been transmitted by eastern manuscripts to the decorations of the Carolingian and later Canons of the Gospels and finally emerged into the round in Italian architecture. From Acerenza (late eleventh century) it spread rapidly throughout Italy and beyond the Alps. A late and very splendid example is to be found in that masterpiece of Dalmatian art the west doorway of the cathedral of Trogir (Trau) built by Radovan, a Slav, in 1240.

A further Italian expression of the same idea is to be found in the winged monsters or beasts which form the base of the projecting archivolt of doorways or important windows. This is a slightly later development and is more common in the south than in the north.

Carved capitals develop very rapidly from the barbaric forms of the beginning of the eleventh century to the highly elaborate types of the twelfth and thirteenth centuries. The more classically minded provinces, such as Tuscany, abided strictly by the Corinthian and Composite models in their main arcades. A more or less close copy of the Corinthian order was indeed general throughout the north, but in the Lombard provinces it was often exchanged either for a type compounded of Corinthian foliage and beast forms or for the historied capital, as understood in France. The former type perhaps appears first in the south; its confronted beasts, generally symmetrically set at the angles of the capital, are of eastern origin and appear at an earlier date at Athos and in the Morea. At any rate, by the end of the eleventh century they appear in the south and in the twelfth century in Parma Cathedral and elsewhere.

The historied capital, or capital carved with figure-subjects, appears first in minor features. The earliest examples are of the crudest possible description, such as those at Cortazzone, and even the series in the cloister at S. Orso, Aosta, dated 1133, are still ill formed and clumsy. The examples in the baptistery at Parma of the end of the century have achieved a respectable competence, but this form of decoration never became a very favourite one in Italy. Monreale cloister (late twelfth century), however, is a highly remarkable achievement and its carved and foliated capitals can stand comparison with those of any of the great cloisters of southern France from which no doubt it was ultimately inspired. It has been suggested, with much probability, that the actual work was done by French carvers from Palestine, dispossessed by Saladin's victory at Hattin in 1187.

Sculpture. The study of Italian sculpture is as complicated as that of the architecture which formed its setting. The meeting of the east and the west and the north is nowhere more generally apparent, and nowhere is it less easy to trace the course of the various currents.

Sculpture in northern Italy was at as low an ebb throughout the eleventh century as it was for most of that period in France. A vague reflection of the revival of German art under the Ottos is perhaps to be found in the older panels of the bronze doors at S. Zeno, Verona, but if these were indeed a copy of the German works at Hildesheim or Augsburg they fell considerably below their originals. They date perhaps from *c.* 1030 and to the same period belongs a grossly cut capital of the Resurrection at Acqui. The revival of Italian sculpture began with the work of a certain Guglielmo who worked on the west front at Modena and possibly also at Cremona and S. Zeno, Verona. Of these the figures on the jambs of the west door at Cremona would seem to be the most archaic of all and may well date from the beginning of the twelfth century. Except that the work at Modena was on the church begun in 1099, there is no indication of Guglielmo's exact period, and his work here has been assigned by Porter to the beginning of the twelfth century, and by Mâle to as late as 1140. It seems in any case unlikely that this work was executed before *c.* 1120. He had as successor a certain Nicolo, whose name appears on work at Ferrara Cathedral, 1135, S. Zeno, Verona, and at Verona Cathedral.

The work at Modena is largely confined to the west front, where a series of reliefs represents scenes from Genesis. The main doorway is decorated on the face with acanthus scrolls with extremely well-executed birds and beasts forming an important *motif* in the composition; a touch of the antique is provided by a pair of amours with inverted torches, and of the northern romance cycle by the figures of Arthur and his knights over the northern doorway. The work of the same or another William occupies the left flank of the main west door at S. Zeno, Verona (Pl. 17 *a*), and consists of a series of scenes from the Gospels. In these carvings one may distinguish some advance on the rather wooden and ungainly figures at Modena, but a much greater advance is to be seen in the corresponding panels of the Old Testament, on the right side of the door and signed by Nicolo. In these the standing figures of the Creator have considerable dignity. The tympana of S. Zeno and the cathedral at Verona, and at Ferrara cathedral are all probably the work of Nicolo and have certain features in common, particularly the featuring of a single central figure—S. Zeno, the Virgin and Child, and St. George —while the main arch of the porch has a spaced ornament of rosettes which appears to be a mark of this artist, and may be seen also on two side doorways at Piacenza. At both Verona and Ferrara cathedrals appear standing figures worked on the orders of the door-jambs and recalling, though faintly, the column-statues of S. Denis and Chartres, to which, if the date of Ferrara (1135) be accepted, they are anterior. On the same doorway at Verona appear figures of Roland and Oliver, and these, with the figures of Arthur and his knights at Modena, indicate a definite intercourse with France and a knowledge of its Romance-cycles which Mâle has ascribed to the lay-singers on the pilgrim-routes. Kingsley Porter[1] is inclined to see an inspiration from Languedoc in this group of sculptures, Berteaux[2] is prepared to admit the semi-independent development of Lombard sculpture, while Mâle[3] places the whole series after 1140, and considers them as maladroit copies of earlier or contemporary French models. Venturi[4] supports the early dating (c. 1106) of the sculptures of Modena.

With Benedetto Antelami we reach surer ground; he worked at Parma baptistery in 1196 and at Borgo S. Donnino, and would seem to have been trained in Provence, or at any rate to have been familiar with the work of that district. His work, on the other hand, is in no sense a slavish copy of French originals, and though it falls far below the greater French sculpture of the age, it is nevertheless a very definite advance on the work of his predecessors at Modena and Verona. The sculptures on the baptistery at Parma consist of the three external tympana of the Adoration of the Magi, the Last Judgement, and Balaam's prophecy. The first of these, on the north doorway, is accompanied on the jambs by a beautifully executed Jesse Tree. The internal sculpture includes two other tympana and a fine series of historied capitals. The handsome bishop's throne in Parma Cathedral is ascribed to the same artist; in form it descends from the much earlier thrones of southern Italy. The sculpture at Borgo S. Donnino (Pl. 17 b) is to be found on the three doorways of the west front. The central one has an advanced feature in the small standing figures which are carried round the archivolt of the outer arch. The doorway is flanked by

---

[1] *Lombardic Architecture*, i. 271.   [2] A. Michel, *Hist. de l'art*, i (1905), 700.
[3] *Gazette des Beaux-Arts*, 1918.
[4] *Storia dell'arte italiana*, iii (1909), 153.

standing figures of David and Ezekiel in the round. Minor sculptures represent scenes in the life of S. Donnino.

The sculpture of the early twelfth-century Lombard churches of Pavia (Pl. 16 a) is of a different andmuch less advanced type than even that at Modena. It would appear to be the unaided development of native Lombard art, and is accompanied by decorative and animal forms which are almost barbaric when compared with the sophisticated ornament of the nearly contemporary churches we have dealt with. The actual sculpture in Pavia is confined to single figures which are rendered in very flat relief; such are the angels in the three tympana of the west front, and one on the north front of S. Michele, and those in the pediment at S. Pietro in Ciel d'oro.

The development of Romanesque sculpture in Tuscany has recently been the subject of a careful study by Signor M. Salmi. The earlier work seems to have been deeply influenced by Byzantine models, an influence which survived till the thirteenth century in Arezzo. A number of twelfth-century sculptors are known from their surviving works. Thus Guglielmo carved a pulpit for Pisa Cathedral (1159–62), which is now at Cagliari; Gruamonte and his brother Adeodato carved an architrave at S. Andrea, Pistoia, in 1166; Biduino another at S. Cassiano, Settimo, in 1180, and Bonamico worked with Biduino. These later carvers copied largely from the sarcophagi and produced work of considerable technical excellence. A certain Guido of Como made, in 1199, the pulpit for the cathedral of Pistoia, and thence onwards for fifty years executed numerous works in Tuscany, including the front of Lucca Cathedral (c. 1235), with an equestrian statue of St. Martin dividing his cloak with a beggar, and the pulpit at S. Bartolommeo in Pantiano (1250). Important pulpits by other hands are preserved at Barga, Volterra, and S. Leonardo in Arcetri, all with marble mosaic.

At Pisa there developed a rich and highly sophisticated art

based on classical models. It is to be seen in the richly carved surfaces of the main columns on the west front of the cathedral and the doorway of the baptistery (Pl. 18 *a*). The ornament consists of the most florid form of acanthus-scrolls with classical nymphs and other figures sparingly introduced. The baptistery doorway has also a series of figure-subjects and busts derived from the sarcophagi. These local and periodic returns to classical art are a feature of Italian art-history, and the importation of cargoes of antique marbles by the Venetian republic after the fall of Constantinople in 1204 is a symptom rather than a cause of a revival of that underlying classicism which was never far beneath the surface of the medieval Italian. The Pisan republic made a similar collection of antiquities and we have noted a corresponding revival in Rome. The most striking example of all, however, was that directly inspired by the Emperor Frederick II. In 1240 at Capua was raised a fortified gateway which has been described as 'a veritable Roman triumphal arch imprisoned between two thirteenth-century bastions'. Destroyed in 1557, much of the sculptural decoration was preserved and indicates a direct copying of Roman portrait-busts and other sculpture in the round.

Turning now to the Romanesque sculpture of southern Italy we find its early appearance in the Apulian churches of the Bari group. The two bishops' thrones of Canosa and S. Nicola, Bari (Pl. 18 *b*), are safely dated to 1078–89 and to 1098 respectively. The former rests on two figures of elephants and the latter on three semi-nude human figures which are rendered with considerable vigour and strength. Shortly after begins the series of monumental doorways with carved beasts culminating in the elaborate thirteenth-century example (Pl. 16 *b*) at Ruvo Cathedral. The accompanying figure-sculpture in the earlier doorways is sometimes of Byzantine and sometimes of northern or Lombard origin. Thus the main doorway of S. Nicola, Bari, has an emperor

in a quadriga at the head of the arch and angels with veiled
hands in the spandrels, while a side doorway of the same
church has horsemen with nazal helmets evidently of northern
origin, and a lintel at Monopoli has a figure of Luxuria,
tormented by snakes, of an equally northern type.

It is hardly within the scope of this survey to deal at all
with the furniture and fittings of churches, but it seems
desirable to note a few objects which are distinctive of the
age or which took their rise within it. Among the most
prominent of these are the altar-canopies or ciboria of which
south Italy produced a special type within the Romanesque
period. These are the staged structures consisting of four
columns supporting a square base on which stand two or
more receding stories with open arcading and sloping roofs.
The earliest of these is that of S. Nicola, Bari, dating from
the early part of the twelfth century; a similar structure was
erected at S. Lorenzo fuore le Mura, Rome, in 1148, and this
was copied at Anagni, Ferentino, and elsewhere. The Bari
ciborium no doubt served as a model for the loftier and later
erections at Trau (Trogir) and Cattaro (Kotor) in Dalmatia.

The great eleventh- and twelfth-century bronze doors of
Italy are derived from two distinct sources. The earlier and
northern type, perhaps introduced from Germany, is represented by the early eleventh-century panels at S. Zeno,
Verona, the later (twelfth century) panels on the same door
and the side doorway at Pisa Cathedral (late twelfth century).
The Pisan artist is probably that Bonannus who in 1186
executed the doors for the great portal at Monreale. All
these doors are ornamented with cast figure-subjects in relief.
The rival series starts with direct importation from Constantinople and is distinguished by engraved and damascened
figures or designs. Amalfi (1065), Monte Cassino (1066),
and St. Paul without the Walls, Rome (1070), are the
earliest examples of the type which was subsequently copied
by south Italian artists. Gradually, however, the engraved

figures were replaced by figures in relief, and finally at Benevento we find a pair of doors decorated entirely with relief
subjects illustrating a northern theme, but executed, as Berteaux says, with a Byzantine syntax.

The Romanesque pulpits developed from the earlier
ambones, than which they are at once more elevated and
more elaborately enriched. The earlier examples maintain
the rectangular form raised on four columns, of which the
example at Canosa has been securely dated to about 1040
since Berteaux wrote. A later development added three
semicircular projections to the three outer faces of the pulpit,
making the plan a semi-quatrefoil. These pulpits are elaborately enriched with carving, and a particularly remarkable
group is to be found in the Abruzzi, signed mostly by mem-
bers of one family and enriched with stucco-modelling or
carved work which makes use of an unusual Islamic form
of foliage. The pulpits of the northern provinces form an
unbroken series, until the work of Niccola Pisano, himself an
Apulian, ushered in a new style.

DALMATIA

Dalmatia was ruled from about 800 to 1105 by a series
of independent dukes and kings of Slav race, who seem to
have acknowledged some nominal dependence on the western
emperor. After the latter date it became part of the kingdom
of Hungary, though not without some opposition from the
republic of Venice.

The earlier buildings, which date from the period of
independence and perhaps overlap that of the Hungarian
domination, form an interesting group which has been the
subject of one of Professor Strzygowski's studies. Mostly of
very small size, these churches are of varied types—the
round, trefoiled, Greek cross, aisled and aisleless—and the
theory has been put forward that they are the native product
of Croatian culture. The types, however, are such as can be

readily paralleled elsewhere in southern Europe, and it is impossible to suppose that a race, for ages accustomed to timber-building, should suddenly evolve, unaided, a vaulted stone construction of some complexity. Contact with Byzantium on the one hand and Italy on the other, with possibly an attempt to copy the ruined buildings of Dalmatia itself, will readily account for all the immediately pre-Romanesque architecture of the country.

The Romanesque churches of Dalmatia form a small group which, while displaying hardly any purely local peculiarities, is of considerable interest as being the combined product of influences from Lombardy, Apulia, and Venice, though the last hardly became effective before the Gothic period. As a general rule the larger churches of Dalmatia, throughout the period, preserved the simple basilican plan terminating in three apses, and appear never to have adopted the advanced cruciform plan of the Bari school. At Rab (Arbe), however, the ruined church of S. Giovanni Battista has a highly unusual ambulatory round the apse. It appears to date from the eleventh century, and the ambulatory is covered by a transverse barrel-vault in each bay springing from crossarches. The plan was perhaps a borrowing from the occasional use of the ambulatory in northern Italy, of which the example at Santo Stefano, Verona, has been dated by Porter as early as 990.

The early Lombard style appears to have left traces in Dalmatia in the east end of the cathedral of Zadar (Zara) and in the two-storied church of S. Quirino, Krk (Veglia), both of which have double-splay windows. The fully developed Lombard style is best exemplified in the abbey-church of San Crisogono at Zadar (Zara), rebuilt in 1175. Here the main apse has the typical arcaded gallery on the outside face.

The influence of Apulia is mainly to be seen in the doorways, fittings, and decorations of certain Dalmatian churches.

The richest of these doorways is that in the west front of the cathedral at Trogir (Trau), designed by the Slav Radovan in 1240; it has elaborate figure-carving on the jambs and a tympanum of the Nativity; the flanking lions instead of supporting the outer order of the arch, as is usually the case, stand upon brackets and support nothing. Although the general form of this fine doorway is of Apulian origin, some of the carving, such as the labours of the months, may well be derived from the far finer Venetian rendering of the same subjects on the west front of S. Marco, while the crocketed capitals of the jambs are pure French Gothic. The staged ciboria at Trogir and Kotor (Cattaro) are obviously derived from the much earlier feature at S. Nicola at Bari. The west front of the cathedral at Zara, dedicated in 1285, is remarkable as following more closely the Pisan type than any other Italian model; its many tiers of horizontal arcading are certainly of Pisan character, but it appears probable that this form was transmitted via the Troja group of churches in Apulia rather than directly from Tuscany.

The campanili form an important feature of many Dalmatian churches and show considerable variety in design. The tower of Sta Maria at Zara (formerly bearing the date 1105) is nearest akin in design to that of S. Francesco at Ravenna, while that of the cathedral at Arbe (probably early thirteenth century) is not closely paralleled elsewhere. Unfortunately the fine campanile at Split (Spalato) has been almost completely restored, but its form again is unusual, and it is crowned by a circular arcaded top story with a conical stone roof.

The decoration of the Dalmatian churches does not differ materially from those of Italy, from which they are derived, but there is an interesting use of the unusual pelta-ornament in the cathedral and S. Giovanni Battista at Trogir, which is only found in the Emilian group of Italian churches.

ITALY

Miles
0 25 50 75 100 125

Mals • • Bressanone (Brixen)
• Bolzano (Bozen)
Gravedona • Cividale •
Aosta • Como • Bergamo
Sessia • Agliate • R. Adige
Ivrea • Novara • Rivolta • Vicenza
Susa • Milan • Lodi • Brescia • Verona • Torcello
Asti • Pavia • Cremona • Padua • Murano Venice
Piacenza • Chioggia
Borgo s. • Parma • Ferrara • Veglia •
Acqui • Dornhino • Modena • Pomposa • • Arbe
Genoa • Bologna • R. Po •
Ravenna •
Barga •
Lucca • Pistoia Zara •
Pisa • Fiesole
Settimo • R. Arno Florence Trau •
Empoli • Arcetri Spalato •
Volterra • Arezzo •
Massa • Perugia • Ancona •
Marittima • S. Antimo • Foligno S. Claudio
Spoleto al Chienti
Toscanella • Teramo • Cattaro •
Viterbo •
Bazzano •
R. Tiber Tivoli • Casauria
Porto Torres ROME • Anagni Monte S. Angelo •
Codrongianus • Ferentino Siponto •
Borutta Sermoneta • Monte Foggia • Barletta
Cassino Troia • Trani
Benevento • Canosa • Molfetta
Gaeta • Capua • Venosa Ruvo • Giovinazzo
Aversa • Melfi • Bitonto Bari
Naples • Acerenza • Monopoli
Ravello • Salerno Valenzano •
Sorrento • Amalfi • Brindisi
Otranto •
Cagliari •

Palermo •
Monreale • Cefalu • Messina •
Troina •

SUMMARY BIBLIOGRAPHY

ARCHITECTURE.

E. Bertaux, *L'art dans l'Italie méridionale*, 1904.
A. Venturi, *Storia dell'arte italiana*, iii, 1904.
A. Kingsley Porter, *Lombard Architecture*, 1917.
M. Salmi, *L'architettura romanica in Toscana*, 1927.
G. Arata, *L'architettura arabo-normanna in Sicilia*, 1913–14.
I. C. Gavini, *Storia dell'architettura in Abruzzo*, 1926.
D. Scano, *Storia dell'arte in Sardegna*, 1907.
C. Ricci, *Romanesque Architecture in Italy*, 1925.
C. Martin and C. Enlart, *L'art roman en Italie*, 1912 and 1924.
T. G. Jackson, *Dalmatia, the Quarnero, and Istria*, 1887.

SCULPTURE.

Bertaux, Venturi, and Kingsley Porter as cited above.
M. Salmi, *La scultura romanica in Toscana*, 1928 (also published
in English).

Chapter IV

FRANCE

FRENCH Romanesque art was as supreme in its day and generation as was northern French Gothic at a later age; it was not, however, so wide in its range and influence. Thus whereas it may be considered as the parent of the later Spanish Romanesque and of the crusader-architecture of the Holy Land, and one of its schools was developed in England to even greater heights than in its native province, nevertheless French Romanesque never achieved that hegemony in Europe which was to be the just meed of French Gothic. The various French provinces pursued widely different courses of architectural development, but there is hardly a province, except perhaps backward Brittany, which did not contribute some remarkable or splendid group of buildings which, in combination, constitute one of the most brilliant and imposing building epochs in the history of mankind. It was not until the close of the eleventh century that France, particularly southern France, wrested the leadership, in artistic matters, from the Empire, but from that time onwards its competitor lagged further and further behind, until eventually German art took on much of the form and semblance of that finer and more perfect Gothic style which the architects of the Île-de-France had long since brought to fruition.

This extraordinary success in matters architectural was perhaps largely due to the volatility of the French temperament which when combined with a violent religious impulse was capable of rising to greater heights of creative enthusiasm than was perhaps possible in the other nations of western Europe. This religious enthusiasm made the French not only the backbone but the strong right arm of the first Crusade, and made their country the mother of all or nearly all the great religious orders of the eleventh and twelfth centuries.

It found its expression also in the extraordinary scenes which accompanied the building of Chartres Cathedral and S. Pierre-sur-Dive, and no doubt many other churches, when all classes of the community laboured with their hands at the common work. It is difficult to imagine the underlying paganism of the Italian or the stolid imperturbability of the Anglo-Saxon or Teuton giving way to such a degree of religious emotionalism. Pisa Cathedral expresses the pride of a conquering city state; Monreale, the luxurious taste of a highly cultured and civilized prince; the English cathedrals, set jealously within their closes, the fiat of a foreign hierarchy. The conditions nowhere were so favourable as in France to the creation of a universal and popular art, and nowhere did they produce so great a result.

The scientific study of French Romanesque was begun by that pioneer of medieval archaeology, Arcisse du Caumont, and since his day a succession of distinguished scholars have subjected it to a closer analysis than has been attempted for the medieval archaeology of any other country. Viollet-le-Duc, Choisy, Lasteyrie, Enlart, Lefevre Pontalis, Émile Mâle, and Marcel Aubert, to name only the most prominent, have each in turn contributed to its study, so that now the main lines of its development are as definite and well understood as they are ever likely to be.

Within recent years, however, Professor Kingsley Porter has brought certain criticisms to bear on the structure established by so long a succession of students, and within certain limits his strictures are not without weight. He maintains that by a reasonable revulsion from the credulous dating of an earlier age, French archaeologists have been led to the opposite extreme of always choosing the latest possible date for any building, and thus, by a cumulative tendency, have gradually edged forward the general dating of their buildings beyond its proper limits. He argues, with reason, that the choice of a medial date, between the earliest and latest

possible point, is at once more scientific and likely to be nearer
the truth. He furthermore accuses the French school of
abandoning definitely recorded dates, when and wherever
they are not in accordance with the official theory of structural or artistic development. On the other hand, the dates
which he himself looks upon as definitely fixed are not always
beyond discussion, and he seems inclined at times to apply
the date of the beginning of a church to the whole fabric, be
the structure large or small. Now whereas the foundation and
first dedication date of the great church at Cluny must, we
think, be nearly applicable to the east end of that church, and
consequently to the major sculpture within it, it by no means
follows that the foundation date of Modena Cathedral, as we
have noted above, is at all nearly applicable to the sculpture
on the west front of the church. The widest divergence, however, between Professor Porter's views and those of French
antiquaries, applies to the dating of certain Spanish buildings
and sculpture, and will be referred to in a later chapter.

The division of French Romanesque into its various schools
is not as easy as it might appear, for the marked features of
individual schools are not strictly confined within their own
geographical limits but appear disconcertingly in districts with
which they have little apparent connexion. One or two of the
schools are avowedly dumping grounds for districts which
have little in common and yet which will not fit conveniently
into any other division. In spite of these drawbacks, the most
recent French classification into schools will be the most convenient basis for a description of French Romanesque and
will here be adopted. These schools are eight in number, as
follows: (1) Provence, (2) Central and Southern France,
excluding (3) Auvergne, (4) Burgundy, (5) West France
including Guyenne, Poitou, Périgord, Lower Loire, and
West Brittany, (6) North France and Champagne, (7) Normandy and East Brittany, (8) East France. Of these, the last
now forms an extra-territorial part of the German school and

will be dealt with more conveniently under that heading, while the school of Normandy can hardly be treated except in conjunction with its larger and in some respects greater offspring, Anglo-Norman Romanesque. We are thus left with six schools, which, to preserve a certain geographical and cultural continuity in our treatment of the subject, will be described from the south to the north, the southern schools following immediately on the Lombard Romanesque of the first period, described in Chapter II.

Provence. In Provence the first Romanesque or Lombard style seems to have maintained its position to a later date than in the other parts of France over which it had spread. Churches, such as S. Guilhelm le Desert, preserving all or nearly all the features of the earlier style were still being built at the close of the eleventh century, and even in the following century features of purely Lombard type are occasionally to be met with even in the major buildings of the province. Such is the central tower of S. Trophime at Arles, which only betrays its late date and Provençal origin by minor features and is in all its essentials a purely Lombard tower. The full Romanesque of Provence was thus one of the latest in date of the French schools and hardly appeared in full vigour before the second quarter of the twelfth century. Though not in itself of great importance, it was more largely responsible than any other school for the type of Romanesque which the Crusaders transplanted into Palestine.

The churches of Provence are commonly of very moderate dimensions; the dioceses are circumscribed and the cathedrals consequently are rather on the scale of those of Italy than of central and northern France. The use of the pointed arch occurs here, very generally, early in the twelfth century, and the structure is marked by the finely jointed masonry and the elaborate ornament for which the local stone is eminently suited.

In plan the general type is either aisleless, as in the cathedrals of Avignon (Fig. 28) and Cavaillon, or aisled and

terminating in three apses, as at the cathedrals of S. Paul Trois
Châteaux and Vaison. The transept at Arles, S. Trophime,
owes its origin to an earlier plan, and the ambulatory plans of
the crypt of Montmajour and at S. Gilles du Gard are otherwise unrepresented in the province. A not uncommon feature
of the Provençal apse is its polygonal external form. This is
well exemplified in the main apses of Cavaillon Cathedral
and the old cathedral at Marseilles, and is carried to a freak-
ish limit in the triangular apse of S. Quenin at Vaison. The
churches of the province are commonly roofed with a pointed
barrel vault supported on cross-ribs and buttressed by quadrant vaults over the aisles. The central cupola, with its
octagonal dome resting on squinches, is in direct succession
from those of the first Romanesque style, and as these cupolas
often crown an oblong crossing, the supporting square is produced by a series of recessed cross-arches, to the north and
south, such as can be seen at Avignon and Marseilles cathedrals. The roofs differ from those of the barrel-vaulted
churches further north by having the stone tiles set directly
on the vault without the interposition of a timber roof. The
lighting of the nave is generally direct, but the small size of
the windows, conditioned by the strong sunlight of the district, nevertheless renders the interiors almost uniformly dark.

The school may be considered as centred in the city of
Arles, and includes all those other towns, such as Nîmes,
Orange, and S. Remi, which to this day are celebrated for the
extent and magnificence of their Roman remains. These
classical survivals had a very marked effect on the decoration
of the Provençal school, and nowhere else in France does
Romanesque ornament reproduce so faithfully the forms of
the antique. Thus the frieze (Pl. 19 a) with putti and swags
on the cathedral at Carpentras and the florid acanthus scrolls
of S. Gilles du Gard (Pl. 19 b) might well have come from
some late Roman monument, while the fluted columns and
pilasters and the classical pediments of many doorways are

copied from the same originals. Perhaps more striking than any of these is the great inscription in Roman capitals which runs under the northern eaves of the nave of Vaison.

One structure remarkable for its singularity and beauty deserves a passing mention; this is the so-called 'tour-fenestrelle' of the cathedral of Uzès, a lofty circular bell-tower with numerous stages pierced with windows and retaining some traces of Lombard ornament.

Central and Southern France. This school is ill-defined both geographically and characteristically, and is indeed a makeshift to include a number of important districts not included in the surrounding schools of more marked character. It contains, however, that great series of churches which have been called churches of the pilgrimage-route (to Compostela), and of which S. Martial de Limoges, S. Foi de Conques, S. Sernin de Toulouse, and Compostela itself are or were the most prominent examples. It will be well to consider this group before passing on to the less important divisions of the school, not only because of its inherent interest but also because of the extensive literature to which it has given rise. The whole theory of 'pilgrimage-churches' and 'pilgrimage-sculpture' is based upon the pilgrimage-guide included in the twelfth-century Codex Callixtinus, which describes in detail the various routes by which the pilgrims from all parts of France were advised to approach the great shrine of Compostela, visiting, either going or returning, the most prominent objects of religious devotion on the road. That these routes and the pilgrims that frequented them were indeed of the utmost importance in the transmission of a common culture admits of no dispute, but that they exercised all the influence which has been ascribed to them is open to the gravest doubt. The whole organization of the eleventh- and twelfth-century pilgrimage to Compostela has been ascribed to the Cluniac order, whose priories and dependences were freely scattered along the various roads leading to the shrine of St. James, and which undoubtedly derived enormous revenue from the pilgrim traffic. It is not, however, the Burgundian school, either of architecture or sculpture, which is mainly represented in the pilgrimage churches, but rather that of south-western France. Furthermore the tributary routes of the pilgrimage served the greater part of France, and their supposed spheres of influence, extending laterally, covered the rest of the country, so that, almost unconsciously, the web of Compostela draws within its limits the great majority of the important Romanesque buildings of France, and we are in danger of creating a vast and entirely illusory school of Compostela. On the other hand, this pilgrimage was not the only nor indeed the greatest of the pilgrimages; probably far more pilgrims took the road to Rome, but in this case the effort to establish the same cultural effect entirely fails. Here and there on the routes the trace of northern influence may be found, but in general the art and architecture of northern Italy remained essentially unaffected by the pilgrim stream flowing through it. It is thus more reasonable to assume that these pilgrimage churches owe little but their scale to the actual fact of the pilgrimage, and their community of design and ornament to their belonging to one school of Romanesque which covered south-west France and parts of northern Spain. The actual priority in date of one or other chief example of the type is a matter of minor importance, for no one supposes that the cathedral of Compostela was an indigenous product of Spanish culture or doubts that its architects learned their art in south-west France, if indeed they were not themselves Frenchmen.

S. Sernin at Toulouse (Pl. 20 a) is a vast church with an ambulatory, five radiating chapels, aisled transepts, and a double-aisled nave, with a central and two western towers. The eastern part was no doubt completed when the high altar was consecrated in 1096 by Urban II; how much earlier the church was begun is uncertain, but the date of 1060 has been considered probable by French authorities. The general structure of the church, which may be considered typical of the group, consists of a main body of two stories surmounted by a round barrel-vault with cross-arches between the bays, aisles with groined vaults, surmounted by tribunes with quadrant vaults and roofs laid directly on the vaults. The round arch is universal and there is no direct lighting of the main nave. The use of the ambulatory is probably copied from that of S. Martin of Tours, built earlier in the eleventh century. S. Sernin was the largest but probably not the earliest of the group; S. Foi of Conques (Fig. 30) seems to have been begun by Abbot Odobric (1030–65) and finished *c.* 1100; S. Martial of Limoges (now destroyed) was rebuilt after the fire of 1053 and consecrated in 1095, and Compostela was begun in 1078.

The system of barrel-vaults without direct lighting of the aisled nave is general in the south-French school, the other features are more occasional. Thus the ambulatory plan is not over common and the smaller churches generally terminate in a central and side apses, as may be seen at Valcabrère and S. Salvi at Albi. The cupolas over the crossing are generally octagonal and rest on squinches, but the round form on pendentives appears occasionally. The external features, including the façades, are commonly little ornamented.

The province of Berry with certain adjoining districts provides a local and distinctive type of church which has formed the nucleus of a school of the Lower Loire in some classifications. Its distinctive features are a wide aisleless nave, commonly timber roofed, and a transept and choir with three apses. The tribune is entirely absent, and the junction of a wider nave with a narrower crossing and eastern arm give an impression of a lack of unity in the design. Examples of this arrangement may be cited at Charost (Cher) and at S. Janvrin.

Auvergne. The mountain *massif* of the Auvergne is the seat of a small but well-defined school of Romanesque centred at

Clermont-Ferrand. Curiously enough this remote highland
city produced a series of churches of the highest importance
in the development of French architecture. As early as the
fifth century S. Namacius built there a cathedral which was
one of the few buildings that Gregory of Tours describes in
any detail. Its successor, consecrated in 946, has left some
traces in the existing crypt. Excavations have shown that this
building possessed an ambulatory plan with four square-
ended radiating chapels. As an ambulatory plan this is the
earliest example in France[1] which has yet come to light, and
that it was known and admired at a distance is proved by the
fact that the church of S. Aignan at Orléans, built by Robert
the Pious, was copied from it, though here apsidal chapels
were substituted for the square ones at Clermont. There is
little doubt also that it served as a model for the ambulatory
with square-ended chapels at Tournus in Burgundy, built
late in the tenth century. Rounded chapels were substituted
for the square ones at Clermont in the course of the eleventh
century, and, thus altered, the ambulatory was the prototype
of the ambulatory plan of the Auvergne which is distinguished
by the regular grouping of four radiating chapels without the
usual one on the main axis of the building. The chief existing
churches of the school are Notre-Dame du Port, Clermont
(Pl. 20 b and Fig. 29), Chamalières, Orcival, Issoire, S.
Nectaire, and S. Saturnin; the three first have the curious
arrangement of chapels noted above, while the others follow
the more ordinary arrangement of five chapels with the central
one set on the axis of the building. In structure these churches
consist of a barrel-vaulted body, commonly without supporting ribs, aisles with groined or barrel-vaulted roofs and
supporting tribunes with quadrant vaults. The main building
has no clerestory and is thus without direct lighting. The most

---

[1] It is now generally agreed that the foundations at S. Martin, Tours,
assigned by Lasteyrie to the church of 903–19, are not of so early a date
and belong rather to the church built after the fire of 997.

distinctive feature of the school, however, is the curious form of the central cupola and its abutments. The cupola itself is of octagonal form with squinches set on the square of the crossing, but the adjoining bays of the north and south arms of the transept are carried up well above the level of the high roofs of the transept and nave, and are roofed with a quadrant or barrel-vault running east and west and serving as an abutment to the cupola. In external effect the cupola thus rests on an oblong mass of masonry extending the full width of the nave and aisles, and rising high above the roofs of the choir and ambulatory. The cupola itself is carried up as an octagonal tower with openings in each face and a pyramidal roof. Towers of this type survive at Issoire, S. Nectaire, Orcival, and Notre-Dame du Port. Another common feature is a series of external arched recesses in the walls of the aisles and transepts, one arch corresponding to each bay of the aisle; these arches are immediately surmounted by the external wall-arcade of the tribunes, the nave and aisles being covered by a single flat-pitched roof. Little is certainly known as to the date of the major churches of Auvergne, but it is improbable that any of those cited above were built earlier than the twelfth century. The retention, however, of such a primitive feature as the unribbed barrel-vault would seem to indicate, as Lasteyrie has observed, that the school was firmly established when that form of roofing was commonly in use.

Burgundy. The school of Burgundy is one of the most important of the French schools in that its forms and methods were carried throughout Europe by the Burgundian order of Cîteaux and to a less extent by the equally Burgundian order of Cluny. We have seen that in the tenth and eleventh centuries the basin of the Saône and Rhône produced some of the most remarkable buildings of the first Romanesque style, and in the succeeding age the northern part of this district was equally in the van of architectural progress. The school of Burgundy extends from Sens in the north to Lyon in the south, and includes also the provinces of the Nivernais and the Bourbonnais.

Foremost among its great buildings stands the third abbey church of Cluny (now largely demolished), which was begun in 1088 and of which the eastern chapels were consecrated in 1095 by Urban II. Of equally early date is S. Étienne of Nevers and parts of Paray-le-Monial (Fig. 33). Other great churches of first importance are the Madelaine at Vézelay (ded. 1104), the cathedral of Autun (ded. 1132), La Charité-sur-Loire, and the earliest Cistercian churches, such as Fontenay.

The constructional system varies considerably in this extensive region, but certain features are uniform, at any rate in the greater churches. Thus throughout the Burgundian school the great churches are provided with a clerestory even when roofed with a barrel-vault. This was the case at Cluny, and with a succession of other churches, such as Paray, Semur-en-Brionnais, Saulieu, Autun, and Beaune. In all of these below the clerestory runs a triforium wall-arcade, pierced only at intervals and quite different both in appearance and intention from the vast open tribunes of the centre and the south. In the greater churches having a groined vault over the main span, such as Vézelay (Pl. 22) and Anzy-le-Duc, the concentration of the thrust on fixed points of the vault seems to have rendered the builders more cautious and the triforium is omitted, there being only a blind wall between the main arcades and the clerestory. In all these churches the aisles are roofed with groined vaults. At Tournus the roofing of the nave, which dates from the early twelfth century, is arranged in a remarkable fashion of which this is the foremost example. Between each bay a round cross-arch is thrown across the nave, and above the crown of these arches and springing from wall to wall is a transverse barrel-vault across the axis of the church. These transverse barrel-vaults are a not uncommon feature in Burgundian architecture, but they are nearly always confined to the roofing of the aisles. In this position they were adopted by the Cistercians[1] and transmitted by them to all parts of Europe.

Following the earlier fashion of the second church of Cluny and the abbey of Tournus, the greater Romanesque churches were commonly finished with a pair of western towers, sometimes set, as at Paray-le-Monial and Vézelay, and later at Cluny itself, on the front of the large narthex. This feature too was inherited from an earlier age, and existed in the late tenth century at Cluny, and still exists at Tournus in a structure of *c.* 1000. In the extended form to be seen at Vézelay, Autun, Paray, and elsewhere, it is a distinctive feature of the larger Burgundian churches, and was transmitted in a restrained and modified form by the Cistercians wherever their houses were established. The crossings of Burgundian churches, like those farther south, were crowned by octagonal cupolas, with towers of the same or a square form above them. Cluny had in addition a series of subsidiary towers over the major and minor transepts which must have added enormously to the impressiveness of the vast church. The second transept at Cluny, set to the east of the main transept, is probably the earliest instance of the adoption of this form of plan which never became popular in France; it was, however, copied at Souvigny and S. Benoît-sur-Loire, and the precise Cluny arrangement was reproduced, on a smaller scale, at Lewes in England.

The east end of the Burgundian churches varied considerably; Cluny, Paray-le-Monial, the extended east end at La Charité, were all provided with ambulatories and five radiating chapels, but Autun Cathedral and other churches terminated in three parallel apses. Two smaller churches of

[1] The Cistercian churches of the earliest period of the Order have all been destroyed or rebuilt, and the earliest surviving example in France is that of Fontenay (Côte d'Or), built 1139–47. Apart from the general use of the Burgundian barrel-vault, early Cistercian architecture is more nearly akin to early Gothic than to Romanesque, the typical ornament of the earlier period being rigidly excluded.

Anzy-le-Duc and Charlieu have or had an unusual arrangement of a minor apse projecting slightly from the main apse without the interposition of an ambulatory.

Perhaps the most important contribution of the Burgundian school, however, was the general adoption of the pointed arch which had become common in the early part of the twelfth century. The pointed barrel-vault of the transept at Cluny (Pl. 24 a) may be assigned to the very beginning of the twelfth century, and there is another of equally early date at Paray-le-Monial. By the second quarter of the twelfth century its use had become almost universal in the province.

A feature in certain Burgundian churches, particularly those having affinity with Autun, is the extensive use of the fluted pilaster and other features of classical origin. The fact that these features are most pronounced in cities with extant Roman monuments, such as Autun and Langres, has led to the supposition that they, like the work in Provence, are direct copies from the antique. The fluted pilaster, however, makes an earlier appearance at Cluny, where there were no Roman models.

Western France. The school of western France, which extends from Brittany to the Garonne, is sharply divided into two types, the first possessing a nave and aisles of almost equal height, and the second a wide aisleless nave, covered, in an important group, with a series of domes. The former type has its centre in Poitou and the latter in Périgord. It is a little difficult to understand why so essential a structural feature as the roofing of a whole church with domes should not in itself be sufficient to warrant the placing of the domed-church type in a separate school, but it is argued that the adoption of domes was more or less accidental, and is an episode merely in the architectural history of a school which began without them and only adopted them in a comparatively small number of churches even in Périgord. Furthermore it is argued that the general ordinance of these domed churches, apart from

their roof-system, is indistinguishable from other churches
of the school.

The domed churches of Périgord,[1] which spread in isolated
instances as far north as Fontevrault on the Loire and as far
south as Agen on the Garonne, have been a fruitful subject
for discussion in the past, and even now the questions they
raise as to date and origin have not been settled with anything
like unanimity. There seems, however, no reason to doubt
the judgement of the majority of recent writers that the earliest
of these churches cannot be carried back before the beginning
of the twelfth century, and that they are of eastern or Byzantine
inspiration executed in a local manner.[2] The chief controversy
has centred round S. Front at Périgueux, which some early
writers, such as Verneilh, and some modern writers, such as
Kingsley Porter, have endeavoured to identify with the church
built in 1047. It is difficult, however, to see, in this case, what
date is to be assigned to the earlier church still surviving in
part at the west end, or to explain how an incombustible building came to be burnt in 1120. These difficulties vanish if we
assume that the church was built after the fire to survive largely
intact until it was practically rebuilt by Abadie in the middle
of the last century. The Greek-cross plan of S. Front is nearly
a replica of that of St. Mark's at Venice as rebuilt in the second
half of the eleventh century, and there is no reason to suppose
that the one was not copied from the other. S. Front, however,
is exceptional, the majority of these churches being of simple
rectangular form, roofed with a series of domes from east to
west and commonly terminating in an apse. Occasionally the
same system is or was applied to an ordinary cruciform plan, as
at Angoulême Cathedral (begun 1105) and S. Caprais at Agen.
The construction of the French domes differs markedly, how-

---

[1] See particularly *Congrès arch. de France*, 1927, Périgueux; also R.
Rey, *La Cathédrale de Cahors*, 1925.
[2] The probable connexion between the first Crusade and the introduction of this form into France is discussed in Chapter V.

ever, from the Byzantine method, in the contour and construction of the pendentives, in the absence of a drum between
the pendentives and the dome, and in the use of pointed arches
instead of round. One of the earliest churches of the group is
the old cathedral (S. Étienne de la Cité) at Périgueux (beginning of the twelfth century), and of which the complete plan
(Fig. 32) has recently been recovered by excavation. It has,
however, been altered by the addition of a square, domed
chancel of later twelfth-century date, in place of the original
termination. Other important churches of the group may be
mentioned at Cahors Cathedral (consecrated 1119), Souillac
(Pl. 23 a), and S. Jean de Cole.

The second class of church of the western school, typical
of Poitou, is represented by such structures as Notre Dame-
la-Grande at Poitiers (Fig. 31), S. Savin-sur-Gartempe,
S. Pierre, Chauvigny, and S. Eutrope of Saintes. The body
of the church, in this class, is covered by a barrel-vault
springing directly from a cornice above the main arcades
without the interposition of either triforium or clerestory.
The aisles are covered by barrel or groined vaults which
only differ in height from those of the main body by covering
a narrower span. Some of the churches, such as S. Savin,
have lofty cylindrical columns, but the more common form
of support is the compound or the quatrefoiled pier.

The exterior of the churches of the western school is
remarkable for its extremely rich decoration; the buttresses
are replaced by single or grouped shafts with capitals and the
side walls have arched recesses in each bay. The façades have
an elaborately carved central doorway, without a tympanum,
and flanked by blind arches, while above them one or more
wall-arcades are carried across the building. Fronts of this
type are extraordinarily numerous, and Notre Dame-la-Grande
(Pl. 21), Poitiers, Civray, Ruffec, and S. Croix, Bordeaux,
will serve as examples.

A local type of tower is also not uncommon: this consists

of two or more square stages crowned by a circular stage and a conical stone roof. Such are the towers of S. Front, Périgueux, Notre-Dame-la-Grande, Poitiers, and Notre-Dame, Saintes (Pl. 23 *b*). The stages are strongly accentuated by cornices, and elaborately arcaded or pierced with windows. A second and more unusual type of tower has its earliest surviving example at Brantôme, a structure of the second half of the eleventh century. This type has a square base and receding upper stages, either square or octagonal, and terminates in a pyramid. The unusual features include the provision of free columns in the angles of the ground stage on which rests the recessed superstructure, and the appearance of a single acute gable projecting from each face of the upper stages and forming a capping for the large openings of the belfry. It has been argued[1] that this type of tower originated in Limoges, in and near which are its most numerous examples. It was subsequently copied at Le Puy (rebuilt) and Valence (destroyed).

North France and Champagne. This school, which covers the Île-de-France, Picardy, Champagne, and the neighbouring districts, was the most backward of all the French Romanesque schools. The forms and structure of the Carolingian age, so tenaciously maintained in Germany, exerted also a controlling influence in this the nearest district of France. The great majority of eleventh- and early twelfth-century churches of the school were timber-roofed in their main spans and even sometimes in the aisles also, though occasionally as it were a tentative experiment was made in the use of diaphragm-arches (Cerny-en-Laonnais) or a barrel-vault (S. Loup de Naud). The interiors are commonly of the simplest type, but in the larger churches are of three stages with a lofty clerestory as befits a northern school. Examples of the normal arrangement (Pl. 24 *b* and Fig. 34) can be seen at Vignory (*c.* 1050) and the nave of S. Remi of Reims, and a later example with the use of the pointed arch at Lillers. At the

---

[1] J. Vallery Radot, *Églises romanes*, 1931, chap. v.

last-named place the wall-shafts carried up to the roof-plate
between each bay show the influence of the Norman school.

Early in the twelfth century (the lack of definitely dated
examples renders exactitude impossible) the school adopted
the use of the ribbed vault; the early examples are few in
number and primitive in form, and must obviously have been
copied from the Anglo-Norman school. From this point,
however, the school of the Île-de-France from being among
the most backward became rapidly the most advanced of all
the European schools, and by about 1140 had evolved the true
Gothic structure which was soon to acquire for the builders
of the royal *domaine* the architectural leadership of western
Europe. This very pre-eminence, however, led to the total
destruction of most of the great churches of the province and
their reconstruction in the new style, and as a consequence
north-eastern France is unusually poor in examples of the
Romanesque period.

The exterior of the churches of the district is commonly
severe and plain, but an early use is made of the gabled doorway which perhaps originated in this school. The plans are
commonly of the three-apse type, but the ambulatory makes
an occasional appearance. S. Remi of Reims appears to have
had four apses in each arm of the transept and a gallery
carried across the transept end, which, as we shall see, was
a common feature in the Norman school. The towers were
commonly set over the crossing, but at S.-Germain-des-Prés,
Paris, two towers are set in the angles of the transept, another
indication of affinity with the German Carolingian school.

The Central Type of Plan. In France as in Italy the central
type of plan continued in use throughout the Romanesque
period, though one complete class of these buildings—the
baptistery—ceased to be erected by or after the Carolingian
period. Even the other types diminished greatly in number,
and the majority of those erected owe their origin either to
imitations of the church of the Holy Sepulchre or to the

military order of the Temple, who presumably based their plan rather on that of the Templum Domini (the present Dome of the Rock) which stood immediately adjacent to their house in Jerusalem. We have already touched upon the great rotunda which William of Volpiano built at Dijon in the early years of the eleventh century; it was copied on a much smaller scale at the neighbouring abbey of Flavigny, and on a larger scale at Charroux in Poitou. This last was built late in the eleventh century and had three encircling aisles, unfortunately all but the central structure has been demolished. To the same class belong the rotunda of S. Léonard (Haute-Vienne) and S. Croix, Quimperlé, the former with four projecting apses and the latter with longer arms forming a cruciform church with a circle at the intersection. The church of Neuvy S. Sepulchre[1] (Indre), founded in 1045, is stated definitely to be in the form of the Holy Sepulchre.

The greatest church of the Templars in France, that of the Temple at Paris, was destroyed at the Revolution. It was a round building with an arcade of six bays; other Templar churches were of much smaller size and of octagonal form without an arcade. Examples still exist at Laon, Metz, and Montmorillon.

The church of S. Michel d'Entraigues (1137) is based directly on a classical plan and consists of an octagonal chamber surrounded by a continuous ring of eight apsidal chapels. Other chapels dedicated to the archangel seem also to have followed a circular plan on a much smaller scale.

Yet another class is formed by the small funerary chapels built in cemeteries, and of these the most remarkable is the Tour or Lanterne des Morts at Sarlat, a massive and lofty structure with a conical roof, remotely resembling the round towers of Ireland. Connected with this type is the series of cemetery shafts called Lanternes des Morts which are not uncommonly found in the churchyards of the west. Finally

[1] H. Perrault-Desaix, *Recherches sur Neuvy-Saint-Sépulcre*, 1931.

mention may be made of the round chapel in the forest of Loches, belonging to Henry II's Chartreuse of Le Liget, no doubt erected beside a holy well.

The trefoiled plan was extremely common in France in the Romanesque period, but though some examples are of considerable dimensions, none have the encircling ambulatories of S. Fidele, Como. Examples may be cited at Marignac (Charente Inférieure) and Montmajour S. Croix, of the twelfth century, and S. Saturnin, near S. Wandrille, of the latter part of the eleventh century.

Crypts. The crypts of French Romanesque churches seldom extend to the size and importance of those elsewhere. Often they represent an enlargement of a much earlier feature, such as those at S. Germain, Auxerre, and S. Seurin, Bordeaux, but as a purely eleventh- or twelfth-century feature they are commonly confined to the area of the presbytery and are divided by columns into three or more aisles. On a larger scale are the crypts of S. Eutrope at Saintes and at S. Gilles du Gard, the latter extending, most unusually, under the nave. A crypt extending under the presbytery, ambulatory, and radiating chapels was built *c.* 989 at S. Aignan at Orléans, and the former existence of a similar structure (*c.* 1020–30) has been recently established at Rouen Cathedral.

Decoration. Romanesque decoration in France is almost without exception either a revival of more ancient or classical forms or a borrowing of contemporary forms from eastern or Moorish art. The former class forms the basic element in the decoration, copied with extreme fidelity direct from the antique, in Provence and the Rhône Valley, and reproduced elsewhere more vaguely and as the work of a man who imitates from a distance or copies from more debased local sources. Such classical details include the Greek fret, the egg and tongue, the acanthus scroll and the acanthus console, though the last hardly advances beyond Provence. The Byzantine palmette also appears, and here and there the spiny

acanthus foliage which from its distribution seems rather to
have come by Moorish Spain than by way of Italy. The
Islamic art of Spain is responsible for a number of motives
which appear sporadically over France,[1] and surprise rather
by the infrequency of their occurrence than by their appearance at all. The brilliant civilization of the Moors trickled
very thinly across the religious frontier and into France, and
the immediate contact effected by the Crusades with Islamic
art had hardly a greater decorative effect. The use of the
modillion à copeaux, of the cusped or shaped soffit of the arch,
of frieze-decoration based on the Cufic alphabet and of the
gadrooned voussoir, are no doubt all due to one or other of
these contacts with Islam, but their appearance is very
occasional. It is only in such buildings as the cathedral of
Le Puy or Notre-Dame du Port, Clermont-Ferrand, where
a number of these motives occur together, that one can argue
a direct connexion. As we have noted before, some authors
have ascribed an eastern origin to the familiar chevron-
ornament, but its distribution not only in France but elsewhere seems definitely to negative this suggestion. In France
it is commonest in Normandy and the adjoining provinces,
becomes gradually less frequent as one travels south, until in
the extreme south it is unknown. In all the other details
noted above, the reverse distribution is observable, as should
obviously be the case in an importation from that direction.
On the other hand in England the chevron-ornament is more
constant and widespread than anywhere else, and there can
be little doubt that it originated in the Anglo-Norman school.
The embattled ornament, though of much less frequent
occurrence, seems to have had the same origin.

The rich carving of the recessed orders of a doorway is
most typical of the western school of Poitou. Here the carving
either forms a continuous band of interlacing foliage with or

---

[1] É. Mâle, 'La Mosquée de Cordoue et les Églises de l'Auvergne et du
Velay'. *Rev. de l'art ancien et moderne*, xxx (1910), 81.

without beasts and figures, or each voussoir is carved with a leaf, a human figure, a beast or a monster from the zodiac or the bestiaries. At Avallon (Yonne) the chief *motif* is a series of large rosettes. Use is also made of bands or friezes of carving, or even of isolated carvings disposed more or less symmetrically over the wall-surface. Such may be seen at Beaulieu les Loches or at Dax Cathedral.

Wall-surfaces when of small area are sometimes also treated with a patterned facing formed of stones cut to fit one another. This is frequent in the west, and in Auvergne and the Velay is elaborated as a polychrome decoration by the alternation of different-coloured stones. The alternation of colours in the voussoirs of an arch may be seen at Le Puy, Vézelay, and elsewhere, and occasionally a double ring of arch stones is cut and tailed into one another. This and the patterning of the wall-surface is an inheritance from Carolingian times, imitated again from Roman originals.

The carved capitals of columns make use most frequently of acanthus-foliage, classically rendered in the south and degenerating into the crude capital *à crochet* in the north. At Aix-en-Provence there is even an example of the Byzantine 'wind-blown' acanthus rather clumsily executed. Other foliage based on the palmette is of occasional occurrence.

Reference has been made above to the intertwined carvings of beasts and foliage, and if there is one feature more distinctive than another of Romanesque art in its more ornate form, particularly in France, it is the extensive and extended use of birds, beasts, monsters, and men, either twisted into foliage wreaths or intertwined among themselves. In its foliage form we find the *motif* in the early eleventh-century Bernward candlesticks at Hildesheim, in the Gloucester candlestick (early twelfth century), and in the later examples of the same class of metal-work at Reims and Milan. In its purely animal and human form the most remarkable example is the great 'trumeau' at Souillac. This decorative use of

animal forms derives eventually from the East and has its
more sober expression in such works as the ivory throne at
Ravenna or in the (Umeyade?) palace front at Mshatta. From
the East it appears in seventh- and eighth-century Saxon
England, but still restrained and close to its originals. The
intertwined human figures appear in later Irish Christian art
and in Carolingian manuscripts. In the manuscripts the
beasts begin to grip each other, the attitudes also begin to
become contorted, and though the drawing is lifeless enough,
the idea of violent action becomes apparent. A still later stage is
exemplified in the eleventh-century manuscripts of Limoges[1]
and Monte Cassino,[2] but it was reserved for the plastic artist to
bring the *motif* to full and active life. At Souillac (Pl. 25 c)
the whole column writhes and struggles in violent motion, and
the same is true in a less degree of the series of bronze candlesticks, the numerous ornamental borders of twelfth-century
manuscripts, and the innumerable carved capitals. All re-
straint is thrown aside, and the twelfth century expresses a
full-blooded if somewhat barbaric life. These are the fancies
which, in especial, roused the ire of St. Bernard of Clairvaux,
who writing about 1124 declaims against these ridiculous
monsters, this deformed beauty, this beautiful deformity, one
head with many bodies or one body with many heads, lions,
centaurs, and spotted tigers, monsters part horse and part
goat, in endless variety of form which appears everywhere.
The reformer banished all these things from the churches of
his order, and by so doing took the first step towards the
overthrow of Romanesque art and the bringing in of the
simpler, severer, and perhaps purer art of the Gothic age.

Sculpture. That the renaissance of sculpture in France in
the eleventh century took its rise in the southern half of the
country and only gradually and after a considerable interval
extended its influence over the north, is apparent from the

---

[1] Laure, *Les Illuminures romanes*, Pls. XXVII and XXXIII.
[2] E. Bertaux, *L'Art dans l'Italie méridionale*, Figs. 81 and 82.

most casual study of the subject. The art had to all intents
and purposes disappeared in Merovingian Gaul, and the
Carolingian revival largely confined its attentions to other
media than stone. The few scattered examples of figure-
carving in stone which belong to French art in these two
periods only show the utter degradation into which sculpture
had fallen before the Romanesque renaissance. There is some
documentary evidence to show that the French church, at
certain times and places, even took up a definitely hostile
attitude towards the exhibition of images in churches, save
that of Christ himself, but that this was at all general, much
less universal, is extremely unlikely. The extensive Carolingian
use of stucco for figure-subjects has already been touched
upon, and there seems to have been no lack of figure-repre-
sentation in metals. Thus the almost entire abandonment of
stone as a medium is in itself a highly remarkable and so far
unexplained fact. In the earlier ages the tradition and pre-
dilection of all the Germanic races was for non-representa-
tional ornament, and it was perhaps only when reinforced by
Greek or Latin influence, as in Anglo-Saxon England, that
they made any serious attempt to break away from their traditions. This, however, hardly explains the general avoidance
of the use of stone by Carolingian artists, who had broken
with local tradition and sought their inspiration in classical
and early Christian art.

The earliest revivals[1] of stone sculpture equate both in date
and provenance with the later examples of the first Lombard-
Romanesque style. The surviving examples come from the
district of the Roussillon on the French side of the Pyrenees
and ornament three somewhat remote churches in the foot-
hills of that range. They consist of the lintels of S. Genis des
Fontaines and S. André de Sorède and the carving of Christ
at Arles-sur-Tech. The first of these is safely dated by an

---

[1] P. Deschamps, 'Étude sur la renaissance de la sculpture en France à
l'époque romane'. *Bull. Mon.* lxxxiv (1925), 5.

inscription to 1020–1, the others are perhaps a little later. The carving is in very flat relief, and, on the lintels, consists of a series of crude figures under an arcade with a figure of Christ in a mandorla in the middle; both have a border of fennel-leaves, which is distinctive of the age and the district. Allied to these early examples are a few others which are similar in type and execution.

The crudeness of the work is evidence of the initial efforts of craftsmen in a new material, and it would be hazardous to affirm that it was not accompanied by a much higher level of execution in plaster or metal-work. M. Paul Deschamps has argued, we think rightly, that this early revival of sculpture is based rather on one of the other arts working in relief than directly on miniature or wall-painting. He prefers, however, to ascribe the immediate models to the ivory-carver, whereas it would appear at least as probable that they are to be found in the stucco-enriched altar-frontals which are native to the same region and presumably represent the tradition of the Carolingian stucco-workers.

These arcaded lintels with figures survived to a later date in Burgundy, where the west doorway at Charlieu (end of the eleventh century) and the south door at Châteauneuf preserve the same tradition, the latter being accompanied by the characteristic fennel foliage on one abacus. The type would thus appear to have been general in the area covered by the first Romanesque style.

From these early beginnings it was only in the latter part of the eleventh century that full Romanesque sculpture began to emerge. The superiority of the foliage ornament in the earliest sculptures over the human figures is reflected by the almost complete mastery in the representation of vegetable forms which was achieved, while that of the figure was still in the experimental stage.

French Romanesque sculpture has been divided into numerous schools, but there are in reality only three that are of major importance; these are the schools of Languedoc, Burgundy, and Provence. M. Mâle[1] and M. Deschamps have shown how extraordinarily varied and complex are the sources from which this Romanesque sculpture drew its inspiration—ivories, manuscripts, metal-work, tissues, and antique sculpture were all laid under contribution, and if manuscripts are largely responsible for the iconography and setting of the subjects, the rendering of the individual figures is more nearly due to a copying from works in relief or in the round.

Languedoc. As the centre of the brilliant civilization of the south, it was at Toulouse, according to M. André Michel[2] and most French authorities, that 'the art like the poetry of the Middle Age had its first and most charming blossoming'. Even as early as the eleventh century the court of Toulouse had begun that avid pursuit of all the colour and pleasure of life which was to end so tragically in the fire and sword of Montfort's crusaders. The rival schools have produced works of a very high artistic distinction, but it is to be doubted whether any other Romanesque work in Europe equalled or even nearly approached the monumental excellence of the great tympanum of Moissac.

The earliest expression of the school is to be found in the series of marble reliefs (Pl. 25 *a*) in the choir of S. Sernin, Toulouse, which no doubt belong to the part of the church consecrated in 1096. The subjects include a Christ in majesty, two apostles, and four angels. The figures are based on earlier models, the Christ being touched with Byzantine feeling, while the apostles vested in togas might well have been inspired by some Roman funeral stele. To a classical model also belong the two winged genii supporting the garland and the cross on the front of the altar slab of the same church. The relief of these figures is flat, the drapery stiff, and the

---

[1] *L'Art religieux du XIIe siècle en France*, 2nd ed., 1924.
[2] *Histoire de l'art*, i.

figures themselves heavy and maladroit. Already in them appear features which are common in the school, the double line indicating the draped folds and the transverse folds across the body, and in the symbolic figures of the evangelists which surround the Christ can be seen some of the mannerisms which distinguish the tympanum of Moissac.

Of the same character are the slightly later figures which ornament the piers of the cloister of Moissac, erected about 1100. The same rigidity marks the figure of Abbot Durand, whose gift of raillery called down the rebuke of St. Hugh of Cluny. The sixty-six capitals of the same cloister form a remarkable series as illustrating the iconography of the age; the figures derive directly from the larger ones on the piers, but the foliage ornament shows a mastery of material far in advance of the figure-carving. Each capital has an explanatory inscription. This cloister is the first of a long series of similar works, scattered over the south of France, which form one of the most delightful expressions of Romanesque art. Unfortunately one of the most elaborate and sumptuous of all—that of the Daurade at Toulouse—was demolished in 1813, though many of its capitals are preserved in the Musée des Augustins in that city and elsewhere. The Moissac capitals are comparatively squat in form, and it appears that a gradual deepening of the capital is to be observed which is most pronounced in the later examples.

The tympanum (Pl. 26 a) of Moissac is not certainly dated, but is now generally considered to have been a work of Abbot Roger, who died in 1135. Mâle, however, accepts it as the work of Abbot Ansquitil, who died 1115. The theme is the apocalyptic vision of Christ enthroned, and, as M. Anglés[1] says, the sculptor 'has almost succeeded, in spite of the impossibility of expressing in stone the mysterious splendour of such a scene, in reproducing the majesty of the sacred text'. As a composition the work is most justly balanced, and even

[1] L'Abbaye de Moissac, n.d.

the strongly marked mannerisms of the sculptor only serve to emphasize and complement the description of the unearthly vision in the written word.

The tympanum of Moissac is followed, at a distance, by a number of other works; the Ascension of the Porte Miégé-ville at S. Sernin, Toulouse, no doubt antedates it, but the Last Judgement at Beaulieu (Corrèze) and the remains of the doorway at Souillac (Lot) are later. The 'trumeau' at Moissac, also with its superimposed pairs of lions, stands parent to the extraordinary creation at Souillac to which we have already referred.

During the twelfth century was raised the cloister of the cathedral of S. Étienne of Toulouse, which served as a Campo Santo to the city. It was destroyed at the beginning of the last century, but some important sculptures (Pl. 25 b) from it are preserved in the Musée des Augustins. These include a series of apostles which are typical of later Languedocian sculpture; they are not all by one hand, some being signed by a certain Gilabertus, whom Kingsley Porter[1] has endeavoured to identify with Gilbert of Autun. The greatest change is observable in the comparative freedom of the drapery, and a number of figures display the rather ungainly crossed legs which, though derived from far earlier originals, are rather a feature of Toulouse work and appears on the trumeau at Moissac. The curious looking-sideways pose of the Moissac standing figures is also retained in some instances. It is impossible to particularize even the more important of the later works of the Toulouse school in so short a survey, but a return will be made to the subject in dealing with the sculpture of northern Spain.

Burgundy. The origins of Romanesque sculpture in Burgundy have been and are still the subject of acute debate which shows little signs at present of ultimate agreement. The dispute centres round the date of the eight great capitals

---

[1] *Romanesque Sculpture of the Pilgrimage Roads,* i.

(Pl. 27 *b*, *c*) of the main apse of the abbey church of Cluny, which one party would assign to the date of the consecration of this part of the building in 1095, and the other party, to accord with their views of the development of Burgundian art, would assign to a period a generation later. The latter point of view may be considered as having the support of the official French schools, whereas the former has been put forward by Professor Kingsley Porter and has received the support of M. Oursel and Mr. Gardiner. The result of the ultimate acceptance of the early dating would be to place the school of Burgundy in advance of that of Languedoc, for the capitals of Cluny are greatly more accomplished works than the reliefs of S. Sernin at Toulouse. Seeing that artistic appreciation alone has so far failed to arrive at any definite conclusion in the matter, it will be well to approach the subject from a purely structural and utilitarian point of view. The eight capitals crowned the columns surrounding the high altar and were thus the most prominent features in the church. We have therefore to consider the alternatives that they were either carved as they are about 1095—that they were recarved or replaced thirty years later—or that they remained uncarved or only painted for a like period. The second alternative is for structural reasons almost an impossibility; the third is highly improbable, and is indeed negatived by one of the arguments of its supporters, for M. Deschamps assigns a certain more primitive carved capital, surviving at Cluny, to the church of 1095 and suggests its place in the ambulatory. This implies that certain minor capitals were carved in 1095, while the eight principal capitals of the church were left plain or only coloured—which is obviously inadmissible. The decisive evidence, in our opinion, is that the foliage of some of the great capitals is reproduced leaf for leaf on vaulting-shaft capitals still surviving *in situ* in the eastern part of the church, and that these capitals could not have been carved after being set up without an elaborate system of scaffolding entirely incommensurate with the importance of the work. The identity of the foliage is thus sufficient, in our opinion, to prove the contemporaneity of the main and vaulting capitals, which must thus all date from the erection of the structure about 1095.

This somewhat lengthy dissertation is necessary in view of the extraordinary beauty of the figures of these capitals and the supremely important position which they must occupy if their early date be allowed.

Work of nearly exactly the same date, and this is not disputed, is to be found in the original west doorway of the priory of Charlieu (consecrated 1094). Here the tympanum is carved with a Majesty between two angels, in low relief, which has the static pose and carefully rendered drapery reminiscent of Byzantine art. There is, we think, much in common between the treatment of these figures and that of such figures as the Grammar on one of the capitals at Cluny.

The acceptance of the early date of the Cluny capitals carries with it the redating to an earlier period of the other work of the early Burgundian school, and the fact that this redating can be effected without doing violence to any of the recorded facts concerning the buildings themselves, shows how indecisive these facts are apt to be. We must assign the splendid series of historied capitals of the nave at Vézelay to the period 1104–20, those at Saulieu to the period of the consecration in 1119, and those of the cathedral at Autun to the period 1120–35. The capitals of the narthex at Vézelay belong to the construction of c. 1120–35.

Turning now to the great series of Burgundian carved tympana, we have already noted the early example at Charlieu. It is followed by the far more important works of the Pentecost on the west doorway of the nave at Vézelay (Pl. 26 b) and the Last Judgement on the west door at Autun, signed by the artist Gilbert. Two other important tympana at Cluny and S. Bénigne at Dijon have been destroyed. There seems no reason against placing the Vézelay example about

1120, and the work at Autun ten or fifteen years later. Both are magnificent examples of Romanesque art, but neither in composition nor effect do they rival the tympanum at Moissac. There is furthermore a tendency to distract the attention from the central subject by a host of subsidiary figures which at Vézelay are confined within separate compartments. Many of the individual figures, however, have all the grace and charm of those on the capitals of Cluny. At Autun also is to be found that extraordinary group of Eve and the serpent (Pl. 27 *a*) which alike for its simplicity and allurement must be considered one of the masterpieces of Romanesque art. That the early Burgundian school produced artists of unusual originality is sufficiently indicated by the remarkable Majesty on a tympanum at S. Amour, which defies classification and indicates that there were modernist tendencies even in the twelfth century. Later Burgundian art is best exemplified in the tympana of the porch at Charlieu and of S. Julien de Joncy (Saône-et-Loire); the first of these displays a highly finished execution indicative of its late date, while the latter in its parade of conscious artistry and florid feeling verges on the baroque.

Provence. The renaissance of sculpture in Provence has its first datable example in the tomb-slab of Abbot Isarn (d. 1040) of S. Victor, Marseilles. This slab, which shows only the extremities of the figure, is yet sufficient to prove that the sculptors of the mid-eleventh century in Provence were rather in advance of those of the other schools. The drapery and feet are admirably rendered, and it is unfortunate that this appears to be the sole surviving example of the local work of that age. On the west front of the cathedral of Maguelonne are two reset reliefs of St. Peter and St. Paul which are vigorous if rather coarse examples of carving; they are generally ascribed to the early part of the twelfth century, but there seems no reason why they should not belong to the latter half of the previous century.

The great age of Provençal sculpture, however, belongs to the middle of the twelfth century, which is the most probable date for the erection of the monumental west front of the abbey of S. Gilles du Gard. This composition is based, in its general lines, on some Roman triumphal arch, portico or city gateway; its details, as we have seen, are almost purely classical, and the strongest element in its sculpture is classical also. The sculptured friezes are copied from Christian sarcophagi, and many of the standing figures partake of the characteristics of the same age. Other features, however, indicate a relationship with the school of Toulouse, and M. Michel has recognized affinities in the standing figures with works of the later school of Benedetto Antelami. A close connexion with Lombardy is indeed apparent in the use of lions as the bases of columns, both here, at Arles, and at Embrun. It would appear then that later Provençal sculpture is a composite art, and after the production of its masterpiece at S. Gilles, its later manifestations are of inferior quality. The frontispiece of S. Trophime at Arles has been assigned to near the close of the twelfth century; in general type it follows the work at S. Gilles, but neither in composition nor sculpture does it attain the same level. The same may be said of the sculptured figures in the cloister of the same church which may be assigned to c. 1150–80.

The gradual spread of the art of the south over the more northerly provinces of France has been traced by M. Mâle. In his opinion it was the artists who sculptured the tympanum of Beaulieu who were summoned by Suger to work on the sculptures of the west front of S. Denis finished in 1140. The composition of the Last Judgement scene in both places (renewed at S. Denis) is obviously closely akin, but the tympanum at S. Denis is accompanied by a new feature—the tall statues which replace the columns of the recessed orders of the door-jambs. These figures which M. Mâle has shown represent personages of the ancient law—kings, patriarchs, and the Queen of Sheba—were repeated successively on the west doorway at Chartres (*c.* 1145) and on the south doorway at Le Mans (*c.* 1145–50), and later still crossed the Channel and appear at Rochester. The existence of certain inconspicuous figures worked on the jambs of the west doorway at Ferrara has also been derived from S. Denis and has been used as an argument that this doorway must thus necessarily be of later date than that given by the inscription—1135. The treatment and intention, however, are so widely different in the two cases that there seems no reason to connect the two works in any way.

The later development of French sculpture in the north belongs rather to Gothic than to Romanesque art and need not be further pursued. Before its advent the northern provinces contented themselves with a crude sculpture which rose little above the level of the scanty surviving works of the Carolingian age. The sculpture of Poitou needs only a few words. Historied capitals are numerous and began at an early period, but their general level is not high. Other sculpture is more strictly architectural than elsewhere, and is mainly confined to figured archivolts and standing figures forming part of the composition of the arcaded façades of that school. One subject, however, seems to have had a peculiar vogue in the west, where it makes a more frequent appearance than elsewhere; this is the mounted figure of Constantine which M. Mâle considers to have been copied from the antique statue of Marcus Aurelius, which throughout the Middle Ages stood near the Lateran and did duty as the first Christian Emperor. It is sometimes balanced by a figure of St. Helena or of Samson and the Lion.

SUMMARY BIBLIOGRAPHY

ARCHITECTURE.

    R. de Lasteyrie, *L'Architecture religieuse en France à l'époque romane*, 2nd ed., 1929.

M. Aubert, *L'Art français à l'époque romane*, 1929.

J. Baum, *Romanesque Architecture in France*, 2nd ed., 1928.

C. Enlart, *Manuel d'archéologie française*, i, 2nd ed., 1919.

V. R. Markham, *Romanesque France*, 1929.

J. Vallery-Rodot, *Églises romanes*, 1931.

G. Durand, *Églises romanes des Vosges*, 1913.

J. A. Brutails, *Les vieilles églises de la Gironde*, 1912.

C. Oursel, *L'Art roman de Bourgogne*, 1928.

E. Lefèvre-Pontalis, *L'Architecture religieuse de l'ancien diocèse de Soissons*, 1894.

Congrès archéologique de France (all recent volumes).

SCULPTURE.

P. Deschamps, *La Sculpture française à l'époque romane*, 1930.

A. Gardner, *Mediaeval Sculpture in France*, 1931.

A. Kingsley Porter, *Romanesque Sculpture of the Pilgrimage Roads*, 1923.

É. Mâle, *L'Art religieux du XIIe siècle en France*, 2nd ed., 1924.

FRANCE

Miles
0 25 50 75 100 125

Lillers

S. Riquier

S. Wandrille
Rouen
Cerny   Laon
Jumièges
Bayeux   Boscherville   Reims   Verdun
Lessey   Caen   Bernay   R. Seine   Thionville
Mt. S. Michel   S. Denis   Neuweiler
PARIS   Jouarre   Strasbourg
Chartres   S. Loup d. Naud   Rosheim

Quimperlé
Le Mans   Vignory   Ottmarsheim
Orléans   Germigny
Chatillon
Angers   S. Benoit   Auxerre   Fontenay
Tours   Vézelay   Flavigny   Dijon
Fontevrault   Cravant   Avallon   Saulieu   Besançon
Grandlieu   Le Liget   La Charité   Beaune
S. Generoux   Beaulieu   Charost   Nevers   Autun
Chauvigny   Neuvy S. Sepulchre   Souvigny
Poitiers   S. Savin   S. Janvrin   Anzule Duce   Paray   Tournus
Cluny
Civray   Charroux   Semur   Châteauneuf
Ruffec   Limoges   Chamalières   S. Julien d. Joncy   Charlieu
Saintes   Angoulême   S. Léonard   Clermont   Lyons
S. Michel   Orcival   S. Saturnin   Vienne
d'Entraigues   S. Jean d. Cole   Issoire   S. Nectaire
Brantôme   Grenoble
Bordeaux   Périgueux   Beaulieu   Le Puy
Sarlat   Souillac   Valence
Conques   S. Paul   Embrun
Cahors   Vaison
Agen   Moissac   Carpentras
Albi   S. Rem.   Avignon
S. Guilhem   S. Gilles   Cavaillon
Dax   Toulouse   Arles   Montmajour
Béziers   Maguelonne   Aix
Marseilles
S. Genis
Cuxa   Elne
Canigou   Arles   Sorède

Chapter V

THE HOLY LAND AND THE EAST

THE intercourse between the East and the West suffered no interruption by the fall of the Western Empire, indeed the reconquests of Justinian rendered eastern influence in Italy and parts of Spain stronger than it had been in imperial times. The Moslem conquests, and later the Iconoclastic movement in the Eastern Empire, by expatriating vast numbers of Greeks again reinforced the eastern element in western art. In the Carolingian age, though we have actual buildings based upon, if not imitated from, eastern models, intercommunication was less direct; the ever-widening gap between the two churches and the general supersession in the West of the older and eastern form of monasticism by the western Benedictine rule both tended to accentuate the division between East and West, and communication was more largely confined to the channels of trade. A fresh eastern penetration is sufficiently evident in the Ottonian revival, but this revival was largely confined to Germany and the north, and thus eastern influence, in France at any rate, in the period when Romanesque art was in the making, was perhaps less potent than it had been for the previous five hundred years. The only direct means of communication in this age was that afforded by the pilgrimage to the holy places at Jerusalem, and though considerable numbers undertook the long and hazardous journey and a fewer number returned, they were no doubt closely shepherded and had little time or opportunity to profit by their contact with an older and in most respects more advanced civilization. It is thus difficult to believe that any of the main structural features of the Romanesque style were derived or indeed greatly influenced by an anterior art which flourished in Armenia or Asia Minor. That the eighth-, ninth-, and tenth-century churches of Armenia bear a close structural resemblance to certain features of western Romanesque is undeniable, but had they indeed exercised a shaping influence on that style it is difficult to see why so capital a feature as the dome on pendentives is entirely absent from French Romanesque art before the twelfth century. In regard to the great trading cities of Italy the case is different, and here it need not surprise us if we find eastern influences at work to almost any degree, but even here it is difficult to trace any element of more distant origin than Constantinople.

With the coming of the Crusades an entirely new chapter is opened in the history of the intercourse between East and West. For the first time vast masses of people from the West not only visited the East but perforce remained there for several years. The founding of the Latin principalities of Syria and Palestine, and the erection of the whole structure of a Latin church in those regions, made their native art and civilization more familiar to the West than it had ever been before. At this point, if ever, we must look to find some definite evidence of eastern influence on western art and architecture. The first crusade virtually ended with the capture of Jerusalem in 1099, and thus any new features we are inclined to assign to this new influence must not make their appearance before that date. Furthermore the largest and most influential part of the composite forces of the first crusade was drawn from France, and it is reasonable to suppose that such new ideas would make their appearance primarily and most prominently in that country. The architecture which the crusaders introduced into their newly founded states, the kingdom of Jerusalem and the principality of Antioch, was conversely in all its essential features a French art, allied to the schools of Provence, Burgundy, and the south, but sufficiently distinctive to form a separate school which has received the title of 'l'école d'outre-mer'.

Apart from certain decorative details, the two features in French architecture which can make the strongest claim to be an introduction due to the crusades are the pointed arch and the dome on pendentives as exemplified in Périgord. Of these, by far the most important is the pointed arch. That this form was in common use in Syria and Egypt at the time of the first crusade, and indeed long before it, is undoubted, and can be demonstrated by a series of still existing examples. Thus while the round arch was still used in the Dome of the Rock in 691, the pointed arch is used in the mosque at Damascus (705–15), in the cistern of Ramleh (789), in the Mosque of Aksa (probably c. 770), and at Ibn Tulun's mosque at Cairo (876–9) and thence onwards. In France, on the other hand, Enlart states that the earliest pointed arches known to him are in the constructions of Ida, mother of Godfrey de Bouillon, at S. Wolmer of Boulogne and S. Wast Priory. The former he dates c. 1095, but it is only a window-head and seems too frail a foundation to build upon, while the latter appears in direct connexion with a decorative detail which he himself asserts is copied from the Bab-el-Futtuh at Cairo and dates at latest 1110.[1] Elsewhere the pointed arch makes probably as early and far more frequent an appearance in the south, and is to be found at the beginning of the twelfth century both at Cluny and Paray-le-Monial. It forms a feature of the Provençal school and makes an appearance in direct connexion with the domes on pendentives in Périgord. It would thus appear highly probable that the pointed arch, or at any rate its systematic use, was an introduction direct from the East, and its distribution and chronology in France distinctly support this theory.

As to the dome on pendentives, the general opinion now seems to be that the earliest example in Périgord, the old cathedral at Périgueux, was begun about 1104. The form

[1] C. Enlart, *L'Architecture romane dans la région picarde*, p. 214. The same detail appears in the Templar church at Garway (Herefordshire).

was usual in the East, but with certain differences, which led M. Enlart to consider that the immediate models were certain churches of Cyprus. This, however, does not weaken the argument that the crusade was responsible for its appearance in France, where, as we have said, it makes its appearance in connexion with that other innovation the pointed arch. The case is further supported by the appearance in crusader churches in Palestine of domes on pendentives of precisely similar type to those in Périgord.

In regard to the minor decorative features, we have already discussed the distribution of the chevron-ornament with its overwhelming inference that the *motif* spread from the north southwards. It is significant also that it appears only occasionally in the surviving churches of Palestine, existing perhaps more freely in re-used fragments and later Moslem copies. This would prove fatal to any theory of its introduction into Europe from the East. That it appears in something very close to its European form in a few Georgian and Armenian churches is beside the point, for it yet remains to be proved that any of these examples are anterior to the twelfth century. The transmission of the ornament by way of the kingdom of Lesser Armenia, so closely bound politically and dynastically with the Latin kingdom, is a simple explanation of this later appearance. It is quite otherwise with the gadrooned voussoir which is of frequent occurrence in crusader churches, particularly in Jerusalem.

The first city taken by the crusaders in the East was Tarsus in 1097, and here there survives a church which differs from those in Syria and Palestine, and appears to be more akin to the buildings of north-eastern France than to those of the south. With the exception of the additions to the church of the Holy Sepulchre, few if any of the Syrian churches were begun before about 1120. The immediate needs of the conquerors were defence and consolidation, and it was not until these had been in some measure achieved and the church organized on western lines (1125) that they turned their attention to church building.

Though not comprising a large number of buildings, nor any of unusual size, the surviving examples are yet among the most prominent architectural features of the country, and the structures of the Latin church were closely imitated by the subordinate eastern churches. Of the eighteen cathedrals, nine retain important structures of the period, while three more can be reconstructed on plan. Their distinguishing characteristics are simplicity of plan, sobriety of detail, and excellence of construction, the frequent use of apses enclosed in square masses of masonry, the almost universal employment of the pointed arch and the absence of roofs, for after the manner of the country the upper surface of the stone vaults was levelled and transformed into a terrace.

The normal plan (Fig. 36) of these churches is a continuous nave and aisles terminating in three apses. Occasionally, as at Tyre, Caesarea, and Sebastieh, there is a transept, while at the Holy Sepulchre at Jerusalem (Fig. 35) the crusaders added to the rotunda of Constantine a transept and presbytery with ambulatory and radiating chapels, as befitted the greatest pilgrimage church of all. At Nazareth, Ramleh, Mt. Tabor, Tortosa, Caesarea, and elsewhere, the apses are enveloped in squares of masonry, and at Tortosa also there are small square annexes opening out of the side apses and evidently corresponding to the prothesis and diaconicon of the eastern church. The Cluniac abbey of Mt. Tabor, now reduced to its foundations, had a pair of massive towers on the west front, each enclosing a little apsidal chapel. This arrangement is exactly repeated in the late eleventh-century church of Graville Ste. Honorine on the Lower Seine, but is quite unknown in southern France.

The aisles rise to nearly the same height as the body of the church, but a low clerestory is nearly always provided, with the windows groined into the vault if this be of the barrel form.

In this particular the Palestine churches are nearer to those of the school of Burgundy than that of Provence. The majority of churches have a pointed barrel-vault, with cross-ribs over the main body, and groined vaults over the aisles, but in a few cases, such as St. Anne, Jerusalem, Quoubeibeh, and Enab, the groined vault is used over the whole church.

The crossings of the churches of the Holy Sepulchre and St. Anne at Jerusalem are covered by round domes on pendentives; in the former case the dome is raised on a drum after the usual Byzantine manner, but at St. Anne, as we have seen, the dome is in every way analogous to those of Périgord and must proceed from the same or a similar model.

With the exception of the local form of roofing, nearly all the features described above can be paralleled in some district or other of southern France. Here and there, however, there appears a trace of Italian influence. Thus the bell-tower at Tripoli is of a Lombard type, and at the same place the doorway has the projecting archivolt of the same school. Here and there also appears the twin interlaced column which is also an Italian feature, but on the whole these intrusions are small and unimportant.

The decoration of the crusader-churches is, as we have said, extremely sober and is generally confined to capitals and doorways. The capitals are commonly of the Corinthian type, either tending towards the Byzantine on the one side or towards the Islamic on the other. As to the first, so much earlier work is re-used in the Palestinian buildings that it is not always possible to distinguish between the true Byzantine and the later work. The Islamic form with its angle-volutes and rows of simple leaves below can be closely paralleled in the mosques of Kairwan and Cordova. It also appears occasionally in southern France, no doubt derived from the same originals. In this connexion a feature may be noted which is almost confined to this school; this is the trick of returning the wall or vaulting-shaft back at right angles into the wall a short distance below the capital. The resulting effect is rather like that of a stove-pipe.

Two instances of richer decoration must be noted, the first on the south façade of the church of the Holy Sepulchre and the second at the cathedral at Nazareth. The twin doorways at the first place are provided with richly carved lintels with plain tympana above; one lintel is carved with a range of figures, and the other (Pl. 28 a) with a very beautiful running scroll with figures of men and animals, which is very closely akin to the carving on some of the capitals from the cloister of the Daurade at Toulouse. The porch leading to the rock of Calvary, included in the south arm of the crusader's building, is also elaborately ornamented, and the inner doorway has a tympanum carved with vine scrolls which is certainly rather Byzantine than western in treatment.

The capitals (Pl. 28 b) found at Nazareth belong to the cathedral whose construction was abruptly arrested by the fatal defeat at Hâttin in 1187. They are examples of the very best French craftmanship of the age, and belong to that type of historied capital on which the figures are surmounted by an elaborate architectural canopy, such as can be seen on the cathedrals of Chartres and Vienne and elsewhere in France.

It is not the least surprising thing about the crusader art of Palestine that its examples, though few in number, were the work of the best artists of the age, and fully in accord with the latest structural and artistic ideas of the mother-country. On the fall of Jerusalem in 1187 the crusading states were closely confined to stretches of the sea-coast, but at this date and even earlier certain authors have traced what seems to be a backward current from Palestine towards the West. Thus certain churches in southern Italy as S. Sepolcro, Barletta, show evidence of being the product of the Palestinian school, and it has been suggested, with much probability, that dispossessed artists from the Latin kingdom worked on the cloister at Monreale.

SUMMARY BIBLIOGRAPHY

ARCHITECTURE.

C. Enlart, *L'Architecture des croisés dans le royaume de Jérusalem*, 1926–7.

PP. Vincent and Abel, *Jérusalem*, 1912–22.

P. Viand, *Nazareth et ses deux églises*, 1910.

J. Strzygowski, *Die Baukunst der Armenier und Europa*, 1918.

lles
Jaca •Tahull •Juan d.l.
•Loarre Urgell •Vilabertran
•Huesca Berga• Ripoll •Besalú
 Cardona• •Amer •Gerona
 Agramunt •Estany Casserres
 Lerida• Montserrat•
 Tarrasa• •Barcelona
 •Roda
 Tarragona

•Valencia

SPAIN AND
PORTUGAL

Miles
0   25   50   75   100   125

Chapter VI

SPAIN

WE have seen how, in the ninth and tenth centuries, the Spanish principalities of the north had evolved a highly individual type of architecture which was structurally, in some ways, in advance of that current elsewhere in the West. We have also seen how Catalonia in the late tenth and early eleventh century formed only a province of the first Romanesque style. With the latter half of the eleventh century came a change which effaced the native art of north-western Spain as easily and as completely as the Normans in the same period effaced the Anglo-Saxon art of Britain. In Catalonia the process was more gradual, and the later art of that province is still largely tinged by the traditions of the first Romanesque. The introduction of French culture and French art into the peninsula, which effected this revolution, was due to three main causes, two of which began to operate long before they had any very apparent effect on the art of the country. The tomb of St. James was discovered in 812 at the place later called Santiago de Compostela, and from that date began the pilgrimage which drew a gradually increasing stream of pilgrims by the 'French Way' through northern Spain. Entering the country by Huesca or Roncesvalles the route passed Puente-la-Reina, Estella, Logroño, Nájera, S. Domingo de la Calzada, Burgos, Frómista, Sahagún, Puerto-marin, and Castañeda. The second cause resulted in some degree from the first, for the pilgrimage to Santiago was fostered and to some extent exploited by the great abbey of Cluny, whose houses and dependencies became extremely numerous in northern Spain. The order makes its appearance even earlier in Catalonia, where the first gift to Cluny dates from 966. Elsewhere in Spain its influence became strong early in the eleventh century under the patronage of

Sancho of Navarre and Fernando I and Alfonso VI of Castile. Centred locally at Sahagún the order soon acquired enormous power both ecclesiastically and politically.

The third and perhaps the most important cause of the introduction of French influence was the series of successful wars against the Moslem states of the south which took place in the latter part of the eleventh and early in the twelfth century. Not only was there an influx of French crusaders eager to fight for the Faith, but on the conquest of any great Moslem city the displaced Moslem population was replaced largely by foreign colonists. This process took place after the conquest of Toledo in 1085, Huesca in 1096, Valencia in 1094, Saragossa in 1118, and in the repopulation of Tarragona in 1116. Thus in the reigns of Alfonso VII and VIII the population of Toledo was divided between the Castilians, Mozarabs, and French.

The court also became gallicized, for whereas till towards the close of the eleventh century all the Spanish queens (with one exception) had been of native birth, from 1075 the queens were all foreign and mostly French. A large number of Frenchmen also were called in to fill the native or revived sees of the conquered cities; such were Bernard of Toledo, Raymund of Zamora, and Jerome of Salamanca. Most of these were directly connected with the Cluniac order. There is a definite record that Raymund of Burgundy, in 1090, brought twenty French masons to work on the walls of Avila.

All things considered it is not surprising that the Romanesque art of Spain is predominantly French and that for that art, as M. Bertaux has said, there are no Pyrenees. One may even go farther than this and say that the Romanesque of northern Spain is predominantly that of south France, for though here and there we find indications of influences from more distant schools, these are the exceptions and not the rule.

There are, however, certain classes of Spanish building

which owe nothing to France, but which must nevertheless be classed as Romanesque. The most important of these is the so-called Mudéjar-Romanesque style which was practised in brick, partly by Christian craftsmen of Mozarabic descent and partly by the still Moslem craftsmen of certain of the reconquered provinces. Catalonia again stands to a great extent beyond French influence. These two schools can be readily distinguished and obviously require separate treatment. As to the rest of Christian Spain the subdivision is more difficult, and though the Salmantina has certain distinctive features, Spanish Romanesque in general cannot be divided into schools. It will, however, be convenient to treat it under the headings of the old political divisions, without thereby implying that there is any marked artistic division between them. These proposed divisions are—Castile and León, Galicia, the Salmantina, Navarre, and Aragon.

Castile and León. The earliest traces of the full Romanesque style are apparently to be found in the city of León. Under the cathedral here, during the restoration of 1884–8, were found the remains of an earlier church terminating in three apses. Though parts of this structure may go back to the rebuilding after the destruction of the city by Almanzor in 996, its general form is no doubt due to the restoration by Bishop Pelayo (1065–85). In the same city the church of S. Isidoro (Pl. 29 and Fig. 39) was rebuilt by Fernando I and consecrated in 1063; to this date belongs the Pantheon of the Kings at the west end, which formed the narthex of a narrower church than that now existing. The church was enlarged by Doña Urraca (d. 1101), and to her rebuilding belong parts of the transept, but the nave was evidently heightened and partly rebuilt under Alfonso VII (ded. 1149). The carving of some of the capitals in the three-aisled Pantheon has a very advanced character for so early a date as 1063.

The general type of the Castilian-Leonese aisled churches is that having a barrel-vaulted body with barrel or groined vaults to the aisles and without a clerestory. If this last feature is present it is on a very small scale. The type persists till the end of the twelfth century, when it is exemplified at S. Tomé at Soria. Meanwhile, in the last third of the twelfth century the French Gothic system of ribbed vaults had been introduced, and this was at first used with a form of structure otherwise largely Romanesque. To this later type belongs the nave of S. Vicente, Avila.

The old tower of the cathedral of Oviedo deserves mention, as it is crowned by a four-sided dome reinforced by two arched ribs of square section. These support the middle of each side of the dome. This is asserted to be a work of Alfonso VI (1065–1109), but if so it cannot claim to be an early example of a ribbed vault as it is structurally only the cross-rib of two intersecting barrel-vaults. It was perhaps derived from the more elaborate ornamental ribs of Moorish art.

S. Vicente, Avila, is remarkable as having the full complement of three stories in the nave, the presence of the triforium and clerestory being very unusual in Spanish Romanesque. Apart from this it is a building of Burgundian type.

A small group of aisleless churches, including S. Quirce (Burgos) (con. 1147), Rodilla (late twelfth century), and Sta. Cruz de Castañeda (second half twelfth century), have central cupolas either on squinches or pendentives. The dome on pendentives is no doubt an introduction from Périgord.

Galicia. The chief interest of the Romanesque of Galicia is centred in the vast cathedral (Frontispiece and Fig. 37) of Santiago de Compostela.[1] There seems no reason to doubt that it was begun by Bishop Diego Peláez by 1078, the work being in charge of certain masons, Bernard the elder, Robert and Stephen. To this date then must be assigned the general plan and type of the structure, and it has been argued that it is at least possible that the Spanish church was the earliest of

---

[1] *The Early Architectural History of the Cathedral of Santiago de Compostela*, by K. J. Conant, 1926.

the group of so-called pilgrimage churches to which we have
already referred, and which includes S. Sernin, Toulouse,
S. Foi, Conques, and S. Martial, Limoges. It is not, however, disputed that the inspiration of the church of Santiago is
French, and its suggested priority in date is little more than a
surmise based upon the supposed transformation of certain of
the earlier French churches. The church advanced very slowly,
and it was only in 1102 that the nine apsidal chapels were dedicated. It might be argued that the same portion of S. Sernin,
Toulouse, was completed when the dedication of that church
took place in 1096, which assuming the same rate of progress
would give S. Sernin a priority of six years. The old church of
Santiago was not pulled down till 1112. That the new church
is the greatest and most splendid of the group is beyond dispute, and the recent researches of Mr. Conant have shown that
in addition to the two western towers and the central cupola
it possessed also a pair of towers set in the west angles of the
transept and subsidiary towers at the transept ends. The
church furthermore has certain details which do not appear
in the French churches of the same group and some of which
must be ascribed to local influences. Thus the eastern apsidal
chapel is set within a square external mass, and the great
buttreses of the nave are arched between after the manner of
the Auvergne churches and those of the Bari group in Apulia;
lastly there is a sparing use of the Moorish cusping in the
window-heads. The actual date of the completion of the
cathedral is uncertain, but Mr. Conant thinks that this may be
placed in the forties of the twelfth century. The further embellishment of the church was undertaken in the last quarter
of the century, and in 1188 the celebrated Pórtico de la Gloria
was placed in position. The final dedication of the church
took place in 1211.

The cathedral of Santiago with its banded barrel-vaults,
groined aisles, and quadrant-vaulted tribunes, had obviously
a great effect on the subsequent building in the province.

The structure of the cathedral of Lugo, begun in 1129, only differs from it in the employment of a pointed vault over the main span and full barrel-vaults over the tribunes and part of the aisles. The cathedral of Túy, built in the last quarter of the twelfth century, perhaps also followed the model of Santiago, but has been radically altered in the Gothic period. A much smaller church of the simple basilican plan with three apses, Sta. Maria del Sar in Santiago, is of the same constructional type, though here there are no tribunes.

Two other churches are worthy of mention—those of Carboeiro and Cambre—both, however, are of late twelfth-century transitional type and have ambulatories with radiating chapels in the French manner.

Salmantina. The chief Romanesque churches of this province are the three cathedrals of Salamanca (Old Cathedral), Zamora, and Ciudad Rodrigo, and the Collegiate church of Toro (Fig. 41). All four churches are or were of similar plan, with transept, three apses at the east end, and an aisled nave. Salamanca was consecrated in 1160, Zamora was building from 1151 to 1174, Ciudad Rodrigo was begun about 1170, and Toro about the same date. With the exception of Ciudad Rodrigo, all these churches have a highly distinctive feature in the central dome. This rests on the four pointed arches of the crossing and four pendentives above; the dome itself is raised on a high drum pierced by a series of windows between each of which is a shaft from which springs a rib of the dome itself. These ribbed domes (Pl. 30 *a*) are peculiar to this district and are probably inspired by the Moorish use of the same feature, though applied in a different manner. The exterior of these domes is not less remarkable than the interior; the circular or polygonal form is preserved and at each main angle of the crossing rises a subsidiary turret. The chapter-house of the old cathedral at Plasencia presents yet another instance of the same treatment, though here the polygonal dome rests on squinches, the chapter-house itself being a square apartment. This is probably the only example outside Great Britain of a chapter-house of polygonal form (at any rate in its upper part) and is perhaps evidence of some English influence. The structure is apparently of the thirteenth century.

Of the other churches of the province only one need here be mentioned, that of Benavente. It was not finished till 1220, but the plan is typically Romanesque, though highly unusual in Spain. It has the five apses in echelon which appear occasionally in France and are not uncommon in England.

The majority of Salmantine churches, being of late date, make use of the ribbed vault, but the transept at Zamora and the main spans at Toro are barrel-vaulted.

Navarre and Aragon. The two mountain kingdoms under the Pyrenees have certain features in common and may be taken together. Señor Lampérez considers that the Romanesque of both regions shows traces of the influence of the Western French school, while that of Aragon is also influenced by the neighbouring Catalonia. In Navarre S. Salvador de Leyre, in its eastern and older parts, has the body and aisles of almost equal height and barrel-vaulted as in the school of Poitou, and the south portal of Sangüesa is surmounted by the ranges of arcading typical of the same school. Both in plan and structure, however, the churches of Navarre are very varied and it is difficult to find any common denominator. The same is true of the churches of Aragon which present an even greater variety. The cathedral of Jaca was begun by Ramiro I, in 1063, to which date perhaps belong the eastern apses of the existing building. The nave is remarkable as presenting perhaps the earliest example of the alternate system in Spain; indeed the arrangement seems designed for diaphragm arches and was perhaps of north Italian origin. The intermediate piers are cylindrical. Another remarkable building is the fortified church and monastery of Loarre. The church is considered to date from

the latter part of the eleventh century and is an aisleless apsidal
building with a dome on squinches over the central compartment. Old S. Pedro at Huesca is an early twelfth-century
building of the basilican barrel-vaulted type of Catalonia.

Catalonia. The architecture which succeeded the first
Romanesque style in Catalonia in the later years of the
eleventh century, at first differed little from its predecessor
either in plan or structure. Its main distinction is in the use
of cut freestone, for the whole facing of the structure in place
of the rough rubble which formed the staple material of the
earlier style. Throughout the Romanesque period Catalonia,
following on its earlier traditions, remained far more in touch
with Italy than any other part of Spain. It had close connexions also with southern France, and in the person of
Raymund Berenger III (1096–1131), the count of Barcelona,
was master of the whole Mediterranean coast-line from the
Ebro to Nice. This connexion with northern Italy and
Provence is chiefly noticeable in the still large number of
purely Lombard towers which survive in the region and
which date mainly from the twelfth century. S. Climent de
Tahull (1123), Sta. Eugenia de Berga (con. 1183), and Vila-
bertran are good examples. It is, however, the cathedral of
Urgell (Fig. 38) which forms the most striking example of
Italian influence in Catalonia. Begun about 1131, it was approaching completion when in 1175 the well-known contract
was entered into between the chapter and Raimundus and four
other 'Lambards', for the completion of the roofs, towers, and
cupola. The church still retains the open arcaded Lombard
gallery round the main apse and a part of the arcaded Lombard gable of the west front, and such distinctively north
Italian features would naturally lead one to suppose that
Ramon or Raymund was indeed a Lombard. Señor Puig,
however, has shown conclusively by other instances that the
term Lambardus at this date signified nothing more than a
master mason and could thus apply equally to a native of the

country or a foreigner. The use of such a term, however, is evidence of an earlier stage in which the masons were, in fact, natives of Lombardy, that stage being perhaps the introduction of the first Romanesque style into Catalonia. The plan and structure of Urgell Cathedral is not otherwise Italian; it has a barrel-vault with cross-ribs over the main span and groined vaults over the aisles, above which are round clerestory-windows. The plan with its deeply projecting transepts is reminiscent of Ripoll, but the subsidiary apses are enveloped in a thick east wall, and the great square towers at the ends of the transept were no doubt inspired by the far earlier examples at S. Michel de Cuxa.

Though a certain number of churches such as S. Climent de Tahull are covered with timber roofs, the normal Catalan church of the twelfth century is a barrel-vaulted structure generally with cross-ribs and supported on each side by quadrant vaults over the aisles. In the majority of cases there is no direct lighting of the nave. The type is thus very similar to that of the aisled churches of Provence, though the pointed arch of that district is very infrequent until a late date. The plans are sometimes varied from the simple basilican by a transept, and less frequently by the use of the trefoiled plan which was definitely connected in the early medieval mind with Lombardy. Domes over the crossing are commonly of octagonal form, resting on squinches like those of Provence.

Three churches only show the ambulatory plan—S. Pedro de Roda, S. Pedro de Besalú, and S. Juan de las Abadesas. The first of these is remarkable for the use of superimposed orders of free columns as main vaulting-shafts, the lower range being repeated in the main arcades and aisles. At S. Juan de las Abadesas, according to Señor Puig, a normal French ambulatory plan has had the main apse-arcade removed and replaced by straight arcades continued to the east and butting up against the outer wall of the ambulatory; this he suggests took place after the earthquake of 1151.

In the two cathedrals which survive largely complete, that
of Tarragona (begun about 1131 and continued through the
thirteenth century) and Lérida (1203–78), the work is still
partly Romanesque in type, though both are covered with
ribbed vaults and display the general use of the pointed arch.
The decoration of the thirteenth-century cathedral of Lérida
is thus almost entirely of florid late Romanesque forms, and
this late survival is also to be noted in the great Romanesque
portals of the thirteenth century at Valencia Cathedral and
Agramunt (1283).

A striking feature of Catalonian architecture is the frequent
survival of cloisters of the Romanesque period, which though
they hardly rival the elaborate and beautiful detail of those
of southern France or that of S. Domingo de Silos, yet
provide a vast corpus of decorative and iconographical sculpture. Those of Gerona Cathedral, S. Pedro de Galligans,
S. Cugat del Vallès, Estany, Ripoll, Tarragona, and Urgell
are the most important. The cloister of S. Pablo del Campo,
Barcelona, has the cusped arches derived from Moorish
originals.

Brick Architecture. Brick was used in Spanish churches, at
any rate from the ninth century if not earlier, but it is only
in the eleventh and twelfth centuries that the exclusive use
of this material in a large group of buildings renders it of
sufficient importance for separate treatment. This group is
commonly classed as a form of Mudéjar art,[1] that is to say of
the art of conquered Moors working for Christian masters;
it has, however, few of the characteristics of true Mudéjar
style, being both structurally and decoratively Romanesque,
while Mudéjar is structurally and decoratively Islamic. The
early centre of the group is undoubtedly the town of Sahagún,
the seat of the great Cluniac monastery and in the neighbourhood of which, at the village of Quintana, a large colony of
Mozarabs from Cordova was established in the tenth century.

[1] G. G. King, *Mudéjar*, 1927.

Many of these were workers in brick, and this element was no doubt later strengthened by the addition of numerous Moorish craftsmen in the same material, after the conquests of Alfonso VI. The use of brick, though not altering the essentially Romanesque character of the buildings, nevertheless produced forms of decoration which give the group a highly individual character and is sufficient to constitute a separate school. Starting from Sahagún the type spread southwards and is represented in the provinces of León, Old and New Castile, extending as far south as Toledo and being represented at Valladolid, Segovia, Zamora, Avila, and elsewhere. Very few of the buildings are definitely dated, but the more characteristic examples appear to begin in the last part of the eleventh century and to continue on into the thirteenth century.

The group of churches in and near Sahagún is in every way the most remarkable of the brick type. In plan they differ little from the contemporary stone churches, but the external wall-faces are almost entirely covered by a system of blind arcading generally in two ranges and finished at the top with a deep corbelled cornice. This breaking up of the wall-surface seems to have been the constant tendency of brick-builders from the earliest times and was later in use by the Moors. An occasional use of the horseshoe arch is observable, which strengthens the possibility of the employment of Mudéjar workmen on these buildings. It is, however, the towers of certain of these churches which give them a highly distinctive character. At S. Tirso and S. Lorenzo (Pl. 30 b) at Sahagún these are placed on a prefatory bay immediately in front of the main apse, the curve of which alone projects beyond the face of the tower. At S. Tirso this bay is broader than it is long, and in consequence the basis of the tower is set back at the sides; at S. Lorenzo, however, the bay is square and of the same size as the tower above, which is carried up in four arcaded stages above the roofs.

La Lugareja (near Avila) is a remarkable building of which only the east end survives. Built in the first half of the thirteenth century, for the Cistercians, it has the same external decoration as the Sahagún churches and the same tower adjoins the main apse. This tower, however, encloses a dome resting on an arcaded internal drum and pendentives, the whole being enclosed within the square tower.

S. Andrés at Cuéllar (Segovia) is unusual in possessing four ranges of panelling on the apses, the two upper ranges being square-headed. Other examples of the type may be mentioned at Narros del Castillo (Avila) and S. Lorenzo, Toro.

Portugal. The Romanesque churches of Portugal have suffered so severely from subsequent rebuilding and embellishment, and as is the case at Lisbon, from earthquakes, that few good examples of the style now survive. The cathedral of Lisbon, founded in 1147, still retains much of its Romanesque nave and two western towers; between them is a deep portico with an open arched gallery above, recently uncovered and restored. A more complete building is the old cathedral of Coimbra, begun in 1162 and influenced by Compostela. It is a cruciform church with barrel-vaulted main spans and groined vaults to the aisles with a triforium. The exterior is chiefly noticeable for the projecting feature of the west front, which contains the main doorway below, a deeply recessed window above, and terminates in a bell-cote. The church of S. Salvador in the same city was apparently built in 1169. The cathedral of Braga retains a little Romanesque work, including the enriched Porta do Sol. The cathedral of Evora, begun in 1186, consecrated in 1204 and finished considerably later, is a cruciform structure with a barrel-vaulted main roof and two western towers. It is of similar character but later date than the cathedral of Coimbra and shows the influence of early French Gothic.

Centrally-planned Churches. Centrally-planned churches in

the peninsula are mostly to be found in connexion with the order of the Temple. Three of these buildings—at Segovia, Tomar, and Eunate—are of considerable interest. Vera-Cruz, Segovia, is a twelve-sided church built in 1208, with a small central compartment in two stories and three apses projecting towards the east. The ambulatory is roofed with a ribbed barrel-vault. The church at Tomar (Portugal) is a polygonal structure of similar character, also with a small central compartment, eight-sided and pierced with an arcade. The central structure both here and at Segovia is on a far smaller scale than the usual arcaded central portion of a round church; at Tomar it was formerly carried up high above the roof and finished with a conical spire, destroyed by lightning. It is likely that a similar structure crowned the church at Segovia. The church at Eunate (Navarre) is a highly ornate little structure of octagonal form (Fig. 40) with an apse on the east side. It is covered by a ribbed vault of one span and dates from the second half of the twelfth century. Around the church is a remarkable cloister-arcade of irregular octagonal form which probably formed the inner wall of a gallery or cloister, of which the outer wall has entirely disappeared. The church itself would thus have stood in the middle of an open court. The round church of S. Marcos, Salamanca, seems to have suffered considerable alteration and the present arcades are not original.

Sculpture and ornament. Spanish Romanesque sculpture is a branch of Romanesque art of the highest importance, surpassing indeed the interest of the greatly less individual architecture to which it is ancillary. After long neglect it has in recent years become the subject of intensive study, a study which is not yet so far advanced as to render its conclusions at all unanimous. One thing, however, clearly appears—that in Spain there was a school of sculpture at least as early as any of the southern French schools, springing from a common soil with them, but producing works which are no mere offshoot of a French school but which are distinctive and different and rival, at Silos at least, the greatest works of French Romanesque art.

In Spain, as elsewhere, stone sculpture is preluded by works in other media which achieve an artistic competence which was not reached by the stone carver till a later date. Such, for example, is the Arca of S. Millán and the cross of S. Isidoro of León, the latter the gift of King Fernando and Queen Sancha in 1063. The earliest safely dated stone carvings are the capitals of the Pantheon of the Kings at S. Isidoro of León, of approximately 1063. Though quite competently carved, some of these capitals reproduce motives of an earlier age, such as for instance the two beasts fronting a fountain, and their general feeling does not run counter to their ostensible date. Towards the end of the century there is a series of other works which are also fairly safely dated. These are the tomb-slab of Alfonso Ansúrez, 1093, from Sahagún (now at Madrid), and the sarcophagus of Doña Sancha from Sta. Cruz de la Serós (near Jaca), 1095. The former has a series of figures, somewhat crudely rendered, with drapery in sausage-like folds, which is no further advanced and not nearly so effective as the totally different treatment of the contemporary figures at Toulouse. It is otherwise with the slightly later sarcophagus, which is decorated with strong, if rather coarse, figure-sculpture which Kingsley Porter compares with certain Italian work, such as the Bari throne and the pulpit of S. Ambrogio at Milan. In any case it has nothing in common with the south French schools. Amongst the figures is that of a mounted knight, which is of such frequent occurrence in southern Romanesque and which perhaps goes back to the mounted spearmen of early Teutonic art. To the same period Porter assigns the seated Virgin of Sahagún, a figure of the static Byzantine type, with flat drapery having certain features in common with the early tympanum at Charlieu. The curious crowned head-dress and the claw-feet to the throne are unusual and individual features. The date of this figure, however, is quite uncertain, as it may or may not have formed part of the fitting of the late eleventh-century church of Sahagún.

We now come to what is perhaps the most important example of Spanish Romanesque sculpture—the cloister of S. Domingo de Silos near Burgos. The date or rather dates of this structure are not yet finally determined, and as they form the chief bone of contention between the various authorities on the subject some more lengthy consideration of the arguments on both sides will be necessary.

S. Domingo, abbot of Silos, who died in 1073, was buried in the north gallery of the cloister of the convent which he had rebuilt, and the nearly contemporary chronicler Grimald records the epitaph that was placed over his tomb. A few years later the body of the abbot was removed from the cloister and buried in a position of greater honour in the church. Now on one of the capitals of the existing cloister, near the spot of the first burial, there still remains the epitaph of S. Domingo, and Mr. Kingsley Porter[1] accepts this as proof of the date of the cloister, seeing that the epitaph must have been put up between the date of the death of the saint and his translation. He also argues that there is nothing in the decoration and other features of the sculptures which cannot be paralleled in the eleventh century, while admitting that such decoration and features are also present in the twelfth century. His argument in this regard would have been more cogent had he been able to cite features in the carving which appear in the eleventh century but which are definitely absent from the twelfth.

On the other hand, M. Paul Deschamps,[2] and following him other authors, have strongly contested Mr. Kingsley Porter's conclusions, not only on the general question of style,

[1] *Romanesque Sculpture of Spain.*
[2] P. Deschamps, *Bull. Mon.* lxxxii (1923), 305.

but also on the actual facts of the case. It is firstly contended
that the epigraphy of the inscription is definitely of the twelfth
and not of the eleventh century, an argument of some weight
but which is too uncertain to carry entire conviction seeing
that almost any individual letter could be paralleled in the
eleventh century, and it is only the general character which
tells against the earlier date. The other argument is more
forceful, and is that the original epitaph consisted of eight
verses, whereas the existing one contains the first four only.
This, therefore, can only be a partial copy of the original and
must have been put up only as commemorative of the original
grave. The epitaph is in fact again repeated on a late thirteenth-century cenotaph set up in the cloister close by, for
the same purpose. On the balance of actual evidence, we
think that M. Deschamps has the better of the argument,
and in his support a recent article by M. G. Gaillard[1] has
appeared in which it is argued, with a considerable degree of
probability, that the church of S. Domingo was considerably
shorter at both ends than the later church (consecrated in
1088), and that the existing cloister could not possibly have
been planned in reference to it. There is further a document
of 1158 definitely referring *ad opera claustri*, which must refer
to some part of the existing cloister. In the actual work of
the lower cloister (there is an upper story, the date of which is
not in dispute) three types are distinguishable, the first two
not greatly differing in date, while the third is of that florid
and almost baroque type which obviously belongs to the
second half of the twelfth century and which we have already
encountered in Burgundy at S. Julien de Joncy. The first
type of carving extends along the east alley and part of the
north alley, while the second type belongs to the south alley.
The late work is to be found in the west alley together with
earlier work which has, supposedly, been reset. This sequence
of work accords well with probability in that the east and

[1] *Bull Mon* xci (1932), 39.

north alleys of a cloister are the most necessary and commonly the first to be built. They would be followed by the south alley and an enlargement of the cloister to the west. The sequence seems thus hardly disputable, and the controversy lies in the initial date, the supporters of the early dating assigning the latest part to the work of *c.* 1158, while those supporting the later dating start the whole work in the second quarter of the twelfth century and assign its completion to the end of that century or even later.

Some further capitals of the earlier type have recently been found detached on the site of the church. They may well have belonged, as Mr. Whitehill suggests, to an open gallery on the north side of the church.

On the evidence of the sculptures themselves, while the reliefs (Pl. 31 *a*) on the piers are obviously quite distinct in treatment from the work of the Toulouse school and the capitals have a flat foliage and animal ornament which is entirely different from the Moissac capitals, yet it is extraordinarily difficult to believe that they were carved a generation or so earlier than the Moissac cloister, without strongly influencing the south French school with which northern Spain was at that time in such close and constant communication. It is equally difficult to assign an earlier date to the Silos cloister while retaining the accepted later dates for the other examples of Spanish sculpture with which we have already dealt, seeing that they have every appearance of a far more primitive stage of art.

This difficulty is indeed so apparent that another element has been introduced into the controversy to explain the appearance of such work as the carvings of the capitals (Pl. 31 *b*). This is the theory that the capitals at Silos are the work of captive Moors. That Moorish captives were in fact at the disposal of S. Domingo is undisputed, but that they had anything to do with the carvings in the cloister is in the highest degree improbable. We know the type of work which was being

produced under the later Umayyad rulers of Cordova; it has
been dug up, in some quantity, in the ruins of Abderrahman
III's (912–61) palace of Medina az Zahra and proves to be
not unlike the best contemporary Byzantine art. In the pro-
vincial museum at Saragossa and elsewhere in the town are
extensive remains of a Moorish palace of the period preceding
the reconquest (1118). Here again there is nothing remotely
resembling the work at Silos. Certain motives in the Silos
capitals are undoubtedly of eastern origin, and some of the
confronted animals can be closely paralleled in Moorish tex-
tiles, but their introduction at Silos is hardly more noticeable
than in a number of cognate examples in southern France,
and we may conclude that, whatever its date, the cloister of
Silos is the work of Christians.

Before passing on to later sculpture mention should be
made of the tympanum of the west doorway of Jaca Cathedral
(Aragon). Porter dates it before 1094, but however this may
be, it is yet another example of the un-French character of
much early Spanish work. The central feature is the XP
monogram elaborately rendered and flanked by confronted
lions and subsidiary figures. The whole treatment is extraordinarily eastern, the monogram reminding one of the
Buddhist wheel of life and the confronted beasts of the older
traditions of the nearer east. It is curious that the XP monogram maintained its place in the Pyrenean countries well into
the twelfth century and many centuries after it had disappeared from the general art of western Europe.

Two other tympana may be assigned to the beginning of
the twelfth century, those of the side entrances of the church
of S. Isidoro of León, which belong to the building of Doña
Urraca. They are archaic in style and one has a representation of the Descent from the Cross, and, like the Porte Miégeville (S. Sernin, Toulouse), the head is flanked by statues with
which it is perhaps contemporary.

Later Spanish sculpture is best exemplified in the works

of the cathedral of Santiago. Here the Puerta de las Platerías was perhaps originally completed in the early part of the twelfth century (Gómez-Moreno has read the era date for 1103 on it, but this is not certain and seems ten or more years too early), but it has been at least twice altered, once late in the twelfth century when the original west portal was removed, and once in the eighteenth century when the north portal was removed. It incorporates work from both these features and other work was apparently added in the course of the twelfth century. Certain sculptures on this portal are so closely akin to those on the Porte Miégeville at S. Sernin that it is evident that the same atelier, if not the same sculptor, worked on both; this is particularly noticeable in the two figures of St. James and in certain other details. It is, however, apparent that the figure at Santiago is rather more accomplished than that at S. Sernin, which would hardly be the case if the artist worked first at Santiago and passed thence to Toulouse. It would appear probable, therefore, that the work at Santiago is slightly the later of the two. The Pilgrim Guide (c. 1137) describes in detail the sculptures of this portal at Santiago, as also the others which have now disappeared, but on the actual work there appear certain figures which have no place in the description and must consequently have been added after the Guide was written. These figures include one of David and another of a woman holding a lion, which are obviously from the same workshops as the two figures from S. Sernin (now in the Musée des Augustins) representing a local Toulousan legend. All have the Toulousan crossed legs and the same type of drapery, and all may be assigned to round about the middle of the twelfth century. The original doorway, like the others at Santiago, had twin arches, each with a carved tympanum, and above the archivolts the wall-space is covered with a series of figures representing Christ, the apostles and other saints. We have thus at Santiago these sculptures which date from the early part of the twelfth century, the added figures of the middle of the same century, and the sequence is completed by the great west portal—the Pórtico de la Gloria—which replaced the original entrance in 1188, as is attested by an inscription on the work itself. It will be unnecessary to describe in any detail this celebrated work, which can be studied in cast-form at South Kensington. It belongs to the advanced period of Romanesque art, as exemplified at Chartres, and is enriched with the series of jamb-statues which, as we have seen, were introduced on the doorway at S. Denis about 1140. The portico is the work of Master Mateo and consists of a central doorway with a trumeau, flanked by side doorways. The central tympanum has the familiar scene of the Apocalyptic vision with the elders, or rather eighteen of them, carved round the archivolt.

The twelfth-century sculpture of Catalonia, like its architecture, deserves separate treatment, for it stands largely apart from the currents affecting the rest of Spain. Its chief interest is centred in the carved wooden groups, many of which are now preserved in various collections, and secondly in the vast sculptured façade of Ripoll.

The wooden figures[1] belong mainly to a series of representations of the Descent from the Cross, a favourite subject in early twelfth-century art, from the churches of S. Climent and Sta. Maria de Tahull, Durro, Erilavall, and S. Juan de las Abadesas. The finest of all these is the remarkable figure (Pl. 32 b) of the Virgin, probably from S. Climent, Tahull, and now in the Fogg Museum. It is stylized to a degree, but the general effect is extraordinarily impressive and it and its cognate figures must have been the work of an artist of unusual individuality and power. It was actually found in Sta. Maria de Tahull and bears a remarkable resemblance in many of its features to the still more exaggerated paintings of the church of S. Climent. Both these churches were built in 1123, and

[1] Kingsley Porter, 'The Tahull Virgin', in Notes (Fogg Art Museum), ii (1931), 247.

the paintings and wood carvings no doubt formed part of the original fittings. The same type is not quite so successfully reproduced in the Virgin from another group from Sta. Maria (Barcelona Museum), a Virgin from Durro, and in the St. John from Erilavall. The group at S. Juan is of far later date and is only remotely connected with the earlier work. It is said to have been made by a certain 'Dulcetus laycus' in 1251 and in it was found a miraculously preserved host in 1426.

Mention may also be made to a series of Catalan wood crucifixes[1] copied directly from the Volto Santo of Lucca, which first became generally celebrated in the latter part of the eleventh century. This crucifix is of eastern origin and of the draped Byzantine type; it was no doubt occasionally copied throughout Europe, and an excellent example survives also in Germany (at Brunswick).

The façade of Ripoll,[2] originally of the severely plain type of the first Romanesque age, was enriched, between the years 1150 and 1175, with a sculptured frontispiece or screen (Pl. 32 a) which was applied to the west end of the building. The general composition consists of a central doorway flanked by five tiers of sculptures and surmounted by a cornice and an attic of sculptured figures. The general arrangement is reminiscent of the massing of carved subjects in panels flanking the doorways of several north Italian churches such as S. Zeno, Verona, and the Italian kinship is further emphasized by the two large lions in the lowest register at Ripoll, which though they do not perform their Italian function of supporting columns, are precisely that type of beast, temporarily unemployed.

The subjects of the carving are mainly drawn from Old Testament History, while the topmost range or attic is devoted

---

[1] J. Folch, *Catálogo de la sección de arte romanico* (Museo de la Ciudadela, Barcelona), 1926, Fig. 67.
[2] J. Puig in *Bull. Mon.* lxxxiv (1925), 303; see also G. Sanoner, ibid. lxxxii (1923), 352.

to a group representing Heaven, the whole composition being a homily on the trials of this life and the eventual reward of the faithful. Señor Puig has shown that this great composition is iconographically reproduced from a Catalan bible, such as the Bible of Farfa, which may well have been produced at Ripoll itself. The correspondence in certain scenes is extraordinarily close, and the use of a Catalan model sufficiently explains the choice of certain subjects which are either entirely unknown or little used in French Romanesque art.

The decorative carving of capitals in Catalonia is remarkable for its richness and variety and is displayed freely in cloister-arcades, door-jambs, and elsewhere. The Corinthian type is generally of the spiny acanthus form, but displays far more freedom than do the severely correct Omeyade Moorish capitals with the same form or ornament. Occasionally, as at Roda, they seem to be copied direct from some antique but local model, while in the baths at Gerona one seems to detect a direct Moorish influence. Often, too, the acanthus is combined with bird and beast forms.

Another motive is the three- or occasionally two-strand interlacement, very freely treated and used sometimes alone and sometimes in conjunction with foliage sprigs. A later development would seem to be the use of interlaced foliage, generally of acanthus-type over the face of the whole capital.

The series of capitals of which the decorative motive is mainly animal is extensively represented, as is the historied capital with or without the architectural canopy. Richly decorated cloisters in the Romanesque manner continued to be built throughout the thirteenth century, and that at Estany does not seem to have been finished till the early years of the fourteenth.

The chevron ornament makes a belated appearance in Catalonia and is mainly to be found in the richly decorated Romanesque doorways of the thirteenth century. Its appearance elsewhere in Spain, as at Segovia, Avila, and Benavente, is hardly earlier. Another group in the province of Oviedo is perhaps slightly earlier, but no example seems to go back beyond the second half of the twelfth century, and its presence would seem to be due to a late introduction from the north which eventually spread into Catalonia.

We have noted above the comparatively common use in Spanish Romanesque of the Moorish cusped arch. This is generally confined to doorways and window-heads, but there is a prominent example of its employment in the crossing at S. Isidoro at León. The occasional use in northern Spain (Almazan near Soria and Torres del Rio, Navarre) and in two instances in southern France (Oleron and the neighbouring S. Blaise) of the decorative and often elaborate Moorish use of ribs in vaulting has been carefully studied[1] by M. Lambert. Its occurrence, however, has no structural significance in the development of the ribbed vault.

SUMMARY BIBLIOGRAPHY

ARCHITECTURE.

V. Lampérez y Romea, *Historia de la arquitectura cristiana española en la edad media*, 2nd ed., 1930.

J. Puig y Cadafalch, *L'arquitectura romànica a Catalunya*, 1909–18.

M. Gómez-Moreno, *El arte románico español*, 1934.

SCULPTURE.

A. Kingsley Porter, *Spanish Romanesque Sculpture*.

[1] *Hesperis*, 1928, p. 147.

Chapter VII

NORMANDY AND ENGLAND

THE high importance of the Anglo-Norman school as perhaps the most advanced and progressive of all the branches of northern Romanesque has only recently been fully appreciated. That in this school first appeared the structural scheme from which the full Gothic system was eventually to be evolved is now generally admitted and its consequent importance can hardly be overrated. In the southern French schools the system of roofing by barrel-vaults was generally in use, and though in Burgundy the alternative system of groined vaulting, permitting full clere-story lighting, was sometimes adopted, even here it never became the normal method. The school of north-east France remained backward in this respect, and it was only when a system of ribbed vaulting had been evolved in the Norman school that it was adopted in the Île-de-France and there transmuted, in an astonishingly short space of time, into the early Gothic style.

The revival of architecture in Normandy coincides with the monastic revival due to the mission of St. William of Volpiano (Abbot of S. Bénigne, Dijon), who was invited by Duke Richard II to reform the Norman abbeys in 1002. This mission of an Italian has been used as an argument for the Lombard derivation of Norman Romanesque, but it can hardly be seriously maintained that, either in structure or detail, the Norman school owed anything to Italy, unless it be the occasional use of the diaphragm-arch. On the other hand St. William, as immediately under the influence of the Cluniac reform, may perhaps have introduced into Normandy the so-called 'Benedictine' plan which first makes its appearance there in the abbey of Bernay (Fig. 44), founded under his influence. This plan, which consisted of a short aisled choir terminating in apses, a transept with an apsidal chapel in each arm, and an aisled nave with two western towers, may well have been that of the second church of Cluny (ded. 981) if the indications discovered by Mr. Kenneth Conant in the excavations of 1932 are finally substantiated. It was in any case the plan which the Cluniac reform, via the abbey of Hirsau, disseminated throughout Germany, and such a church as S. Nicholas at Caen is very close in its planning to a number of churches of the Hirsau school.

Though this plan was by far the most usual in the abbeys of Normandy, it was not the only one adopted, for recent excavations have shown that both the cathedral of Rouen (begun c. 1025) and the abbey of Jumièges (1040–67) had a fully developed ambulatory plan with radiating chapels (at any rate at Rouen), no doubt derived from the adjoining provinces on the south where this type of building had already established itself.

It is, however, in their general structure that the eleventh-century Norman churches are most significant. From the earliest surviving example at Bernay (1017–c. 1050) (Pl. 33 b) onwards all the major buildings were provided with a fully developed triforium and clerestory, and the bays were generally divided by wall-shafts extending from the floor up-wards. It has been argued, with great probability, that these shafts imply at any rate the idea of roofing the main spans of the building with a groined vault springing from the shafts, though this intention was not actually effected till after the middle of the century. The question is somewhat compli-cated by the known employment, in at any rate two instances, of the diaphragm-arch as used in northern Italy at the same period, for the wall-shafts would serve equally well for the support of these arches. The diaphragm-arch was commonly sprung across the building between alternate bays only, and as in Italy may have been the preliminary step towards placing a stone vault over the double bay. The original arrangement of the clerestory windows in the nave of S. Étienne, Caen (1064–73), perhaps implies that such a vault was actually constructed there, which would serve as a useful precedent for the design for a similar roof over the Emperor Henry IV's church at Speyer (*c.* 1100) and the rather later nave at Mainz. The logical result of the adoption of this system is the employment of the alternating heavy and simple pier, which, however, does not appear at S. Étienne, but is to be found on the other hand at Jumièges (Pl. 33 *a*), where no such vault was ever erected, though a system of diaphragm-arches may well have been employed. Jumièges is of great importance, however, as the prototype of the alternating piers of the cathedral of Durham and the churches deriving from it. Normally, and particularly in the earlier examples, the wall-shafts are carried up the wall to finish ineffectively at the roof-plate, either through inexperience or lack of faith in the stability of the structure, and this illogical arrangement was transmitted and reproduced in many of the greater churches of England.

The adoption of the groined vault in place of the barrel-vaults of the southern provinces was almost as much a necessity in Normandy as in England, as only thus could the necessary amount of lighting be obtained through the clerestory.

An unusual feature was present in many or most of the early Norman churches, in the stone gallery carried across the ends of the transepts or even over the whole arm up to the crossing. These galleries formed a useful means of communication with the upper chapels which commonly surmounted the apses east of the transept. The very complete twelfth-century church at S. Georges de Boscherville retains this arrangement intact and traces can be seen in several English churches, though at Winchester alone does the actual gallery survive.

The introduction of Norman Romanesque into England was begun by Edward the Confessor with the building of the abbey church at Westminster (*c.* 1045–50). Sufficient remains of this building have from time to time come to light to show that it was of the three-apse Norman type and had a nave with the alternating piers of Jumièges. It was, however, on a much larger scale than the contemporary Norman churches, the nave being of twelve bays (or six double bays) and terminating in a pair of towers. Shortly after the Conquest the rebuilding of the great majority of the cathedral and abbey churches of England was undertaken, and about half of these followed the three-apse type of Westminster. Such were the cathedrals of Canterbury (begun 1070–1), Old Sarum (1075–8), Lincoln (begun 1072–3), Durham (begun 1093), and the abbey churches of St. Albans (Pl. 34 *a*), Ely, St. Mary, York, &c. The other early Anglo-Norman churches followed the ambulatory type of plan, and of these the earliest was the Conqueror's own abbey church at Battle (begun 1070–1). This abbey was colonized by monks from Marmoutier by Tours who are said to have had some concern with the actual building. If so they may well have adopted the type of plan already usual in that district, though the type might equally well have been copied from Rouen Cathedral or Jumièges. The same plan was employed at the cathedrals of Winchester (begun 1079), Worcester (begun 1084), Chichester (begun *c.* 1095), Norwich (begun 1096), and in the abbeys of St. Augustine, Canterbury (begun *c.* 1072), Gloucester (Fig. 43, begun 1089), Tewkesbury (after 1087), &c.

Following in the steps of the Confessor's architect many of these churches were designed on a scale far larger than was usual in Normandy, the nave at Norwich extending to fourteen bays and numerous others being almost equally extensive. The plan too was often elaborated, a type with seven eastern chapels, set in echelon to the east of the choir and transept, being adopted at St. Albans, St. Mary, York, Binham, and perhaps elsewhere. The Norman system of a central and two western towers, though usual, was not universal in England.

Thus towers over the transepts were probably erected at Old Sarum in the eleventh century and were copied at Exeter in the following century; at Winchester subsidiary towers were designed over the four outer angles of the transept, though they were never completed, and at Hereford two towers were designed and probably built over the east ends of the choir-aisles, a touch of German Romanesque perhaps due to the nationality of the mid eleventh-century bishops who came from Lorraine. The most distinctively English tower-system, however, is that formerly exemplified at Ely, where the two towers were placed axially over the crossing and at the west end of the church. This system was no doubt an inheritance from Anglo-Saxon times and through them, ultimately, from a Carolingian original. Such towers are known from documentary sources to have existed in the pre-Conquest churches at Durham and Ramsey, and there is evidence of the same arrangement on a smaller scale at Deerhurst and Dover (St. Mary in Castro). After the Conquest such axial towers were apparently erected at Bury and Winchester, and no doubt elsewhere, in addition to Ely. Of all the eleventh-century Norman towers in England the only important example still surviving is that at St. Albans; many of the others fell owing to faulty foundations and the rest were subsequently rebuilt or extensively altered.

The system of groined vaulting produced in Normandy in the second half of the eleventh century was introduced also into England, but unfortunately not a single example of its employment over the main span of a major building has survived. The system of butting arches over the triforia at Norwich and Chichester and the quadrant vault over the choir triforium at Gloucester show that in each of these cases such a vault was intended and perhaps achieved, and there is evidence that a vault was also erected over the nave at Gloucester. The clearest evidence, however, is in the nave at Chepstow Priory, where the actual cutting back of the former vault can yet be seen. In general the Anglo-Norman architect seems to have devoted his energies to scale rather than construction, and the great majority of his works were always intended to be roofed in timber.

It is thus rather difficult to understand the production of the great church at Durham (Pl. 35 *b*, and Fig. 42), which in the matter of vaulting forms a landmark of the highest importance in the history not only of Anglo-Norman but of European Romanesque. Here for the first time, outside Lombardy, was produced a great church designed from the first to be completely roofed with a system of ribbed vaults. The history of the construction has been conclusively established by Dr. John Bilson, and from this it appears that from the beginning of the church in 1093 it was designed to receive this covering, thus anticipating any other example in the Anglo-Norman school and, by a much longer period, any example in the Île-de-France. Ribbed vaulting was also adopted, in the early years of the twelfth century, at Winchester, Peterborough, and elsewhere.

The structural system at Durham of the alternating cylindrical and heavy or compound pier was no doubt derived from the similar system employed at Jumièges and at the Confessor's church at Westminster. Durham itself was closely copied at Lindisfarne Priory and at Waltham.

With the early years of the twelfth century a number of new types appear in English Romanesque, which show the general tendency to return to the square east end which seems to have always been more acceptable to English taste than the apsidal termination reintroduced from Normandy. In the type exemplified at Hereford (*c.* 1115) and St. John's, Chester, the apses seem to have been still retained, but the central one was greatly reduced in height and was entered by a comparatively low arch in the square east end of the main building. In the second type, exemplified at Romsey (*c.* 1120) (Fig. 46), the ambulatory was retained but carried round a square east end and opened into chapels projecting to the east of it. In the third type (e.g. Southwell Minster, c. 1120, Fig. 45) the main building terminated in a square-ended presbytery with aisles stopping short a bay to the west.

To the early part of the twelfth century also belongs the remarkable group of west country naves which are distinguished by the use of the exaggerated cylindrical column, of such height as to dwarf both the triforium and clerestory and of a diameter of some 6 feet. The earliest surviving examples are at Gloucester (Pl. 35 a) and Tewkesbury, and there are remains of the same system at Pershore. The use of the lofty cylindrical column in a continuous arcade makes an occasional appearance in both France and Italy (e.g. S. Savin-sur-Gartempe, Tournus, S. Abbondio, Como, &c.), but in a totally dissimilar context, and the Gloucester type must be considered as a purely local product. Tewkesbury is further remarkable for the now unique design of its west front, the main feature of which is an enormous arched recess extending up into the gable. Foundations indicate that a similar arrangement was adopted also in John de Vilula's cathedral at Bath.

After the completion of the nave-vault at Durham (c. 1130), where the pointed arch appears for the first time in English Romanesque, the school seems to have made little or no structural advance for a considerable period, perhaps owing to the disturbed condition of the kingdom during the Great Anarchy. In Normandy, on the other hand, considerable strides were made in the elaboration and perfecting of the ribbed vault. Two new types made their appearance c. 1130, the more primitive being that adopted at the Trinité, Caen. This vault is a quadripartite ribbed vault over the double bay, reinforced by what is practically a diaphragm-arch over the intermediate pier. It is evident that this is an experimental stage in the production of a true sexpartite vault which was in fact constructed over the nave at S. Étienne, Caen, at very nearly the same date.

Several important towers of the English twelfth-century churches still survive and display a considerable elaboration of arcading and other enrichments. The central towers of Tewkesbury and Norwich are well-known examples, while Southwell retains its full complement of three towers but little altered. The elaboration of the west front was a frequent feature of these later English churches. The placing of the western towers beyond the limits of the aisles was perhaps first adopted at St. Botolph, Colchester, but a much more elaborate scheme was adopted in two great churches with a single western tower. At both Ely and Bury St. Edmunds a west transept was constructed, which in the latter case with its attendant chapels had a lateral spread of about 250 feet. Unfortunately only masses of rubble core, built into a house, now survive of this remarkable structure, but at Ely the western tower and one arm of the transept are still standing.

With the introduction of the Cistercian order into England began the gradual decline of English Romanesque. In the second half of the twelfth century numerous churches were built or rebuilt in which the conflicting elements of florid Romanesque and early Gothic can be seen side by side. The building of the early French Gothic choir at Canterbury (1174–84) had not, however, the effect that might have been expected, and English architecture pursued its course of gradual development largely unaffected by this demonstration of a greatly superior structure in its midst. Down to almost the end of the twelfth century churches continued to be built which were in form and structure almost purely Romanesque, and forms of Romanesque ornament survived even into the thirteenth century.

Centrally planned Churches. A revival of the central type of plan was introduced into England shortly before the Conquest by Abbot Wulfric at St. Augustine's, Canterbury. He seems to have been inspired by the building of William of Volpiano's rotunda at Dijon, and the walls of the lowest story of his uncompleted structure have been uncovered by excavation.

Anglo-Norman churches of the type in England are generally connected either with the two great military orders of the Temple and the Hospital or with the dedication to St. Sepulchre. In either case their construction is directly attributable to the Crusades. The ordinary type, of which three examples survive (at Northampton, Cambridge, and the Temple, London; Little Maplestead is a fourteenth-century copy), has a circular nave with an arcade of six or eight bays standing within it. An example of an alternative type without the arcade and roofed in one span still exists at Ludlow Castle. The former existence of a number of other examples has been demonstrated by excavation or from documentary sources; the total number (fifteen in all), however, was not great.

In quite a different class are the two Gloucestershire village churches of Ozleworth and Swindon, where there still exist hexagonal structures which did duty as towers and had either a chancel only or a nave and chancel to the east of them.

A third class is provided by a single example at Hereford, where the Bishop's chapel, built late in the eleventh century and mostly pulled down in the eighteenth, reproduced all the features of the 'double-chapels' of Germany, which will be more fully referred to in a later chapter.

The trefoiled plan with apses to the east, north, and south, so far as we know, makes no appearance in England, though there is an eleventh-century example at S. Saturnin, near St. Wandrille, in Normandy.

Crypts. The crypts of the late eleventh-century Anglo-Norman churches form a much more prominent feature than do the corresponding features in Normandy. Recent excavations have proved that an extensive ambulatory crypt was built under the early eleventh-century cathedral at Rouen, but elsewhere in the duchy the much smaller crypts at Bayeux Cathedral and the Trinité at Caen are the only important examples, and the latter is necessitated by the heavy fall in the ground-level at the east end of the church. In England, on the other hand, a considerable number of the early churches, though built on nearly level sites, were provided with eastern crypts often of large size. Thus we know that the two great churches at Canterbury, Winchester, Worcester, Old St. Paul's, Gloucester, Evesham, and Bury, all in the southern part of the country and all dating from the eleventh century, were so provided. With the exception of Canterbury Cathedral, nearly all these crypts were built on the ambulatory plan, and at Canterbury itself the early crypt was soon enlarged into the same form, together with the church above it. It is a rather remarkable fact that no great church built *de novo* in the first half of the twelfth century seems to have been so supplied, unless this be the date of the earlier parts of the crypt at Rochester. After the middle of the century, however, a great crypt was constructed by Archbishop Roger under his new choir at York.

The curious arrangement of the three small crypts at Christchurch (Hants), underlying the choir and the two ends of the transept, deserves a passing notice as a feature not elsewhere exemplified.

Ornament. The ornament of the eleventh-century churches of both Normandy and England is extremely meagre both in extent and variety. The decoration of arches and mouldings is confined to the simple billet ornament and a diapered decoration resembling chip-carving. The normal Norman capital is decorated with one or more ranges of leaves in the form of simple volutes or crockets and this form is not uncommon also in England. In this country, however, its place is largely taken by the cushion-capital which is almost if not quite unknown in Normandy. The introduction of the cushion-capital into England appears to have preceded the Conquest by a few years and to have come from Germany, where it had firmly established itself in the second quarter of the eleventh century. While in Germany, however, the cushion-capital was retained in its simple form throughout the Romanesque period, in England its rather rude and clumsy outline was soon cut up and subdivided to produce that derived form the scalloped or gadrooned capital, this process beginning well before the end of the eleventh century. The occasional appearance of figure-carving in these early Norman churches, as at Bernay and Durham Castle chapel, only serves to show how entirely untrained and barbaric were the Norman masons in the art of sculpture.

The rich geometrical decoration which is particularly distinctive of Anglo-Norman Romanesque began to make its appearance in the early years of the twelfth century, and it is possible very closely to date the introduction of the most typical of all these ornaments—the chevron—to the decade between 1110 and 1120. It must be understood that the Romanesque chevron-ornament consists essentially of the breaking of the mouldings of an arch or string-course into a zigzag (hence the descriptive French *bâton brisé*), and as such may not be confounded with the decorative use of the zigzag *motif* in other forms which occurs at all times and in all places. The few writers who have touched upon the origin and distribution of this *motif* are not in accord in their conclusions. Thus Enlart was evidently inclined to attribute it to an Islamic source, while Gál seems to look upon it as belonging to the common stock of European Romanesque. A careful examination, however, of its distribution leads one to a very definite conclusion, which is not at variance with the chronological data of the individual examples. As we have said, it makes its appearance in England about or soon after the year 1110, and the earliest examples in France cannot reasonably be placed at any earlier date, whilst elsewhere the *motif* makes a more belated appearance. Its introduction would thus just permit of the theory of a transmission by the returning hosts of the first crusade, if it could be shown that earlier

examples could be met with in the Islamic buildings of Syria
and Egypt. This, however, is not the case, for though Enlart
cites the Bab el Futtuh at Cairo as an earlier instance, this
gate displays only a lozenge diapered ornament on a flat
surface, which has no bearing on the subject.

On the other hand the European distribution of chevron-
ornament, which we have already touched upon in individual
countries, is highly significant. In England it is universal and
ubiquitous both in the major and minor churches, the individual examples running probably into many hundreds if not
thousands. In Normandy it is quite common, if not so
frequent as in England, and there are numerous examples
elsewhere in northern France. Going southwards, however,
the examples, as we have seen, become less and less frequent,
until they die out almost altogether in the southern part of
the country. The scattered examples in Spain would all
appear to date from the second half of the twelfth century and
even later. Northern Italy also produces perhaps half a dozen
examples and they are equally rare in Germany. The examples
in Norway may be safely ascribed to English influence, and
the odd instances in Hungary and Austria to isolated masons
from almost any quarter. Of more significance is the marked
favour of the *motif* in Sicily and a part of the Duchy of Apulia,
where it lingered on into the fourteenth century. This distribution clearly indicates the origin of the ornament in the
Anglo-Norman school, its transmission thence directly by the
Norman conquerors into Sicily and Apulia, and its gradual
dissemination over the other parts of Europe and in occasional
instances to the Crusader buildings of Palestine.

The other decorative motives of the school—the embattled
ornament, the cable, the disk, the beak-head, the reel, and
others—all make their appearance shortly after the chevron
and Anglo-Norman Romanesque reached its maximum stage
of enrichment before the middle of the twelfth century. The
beak-head deserves a few words as being almost certainly the

production of the English branch of the school. Derived without doubt from earlier Scandinavian ornament, this rather barbaric *motif* was adopted very generally in English Romanesque, and also makes its appearance far less generally in Normandy and the adjoining districts. Elsewhere it seems to be almost unknown. None of these Anglo-Norman enrichments seems to be at all localized in England or to be peculiar to any district. There is, however, a remarkable school of decoration, including both geometrical forms and figures, which makes its appearance in Herefordshire (Pl. 37 *b*) in the first half of the twelfth century and forms a definite local school. It is tinged with both Scandinavian and Celtic feeling, and its individual examples are so closely akin that they must have been the product of the same workshop. Kilpeck, Shobdon (dedicated before 1148), and the west doorway at Leominster are the best known examples.

Sculpture. The study of Romanesque sculpture in England is a complicated one, owing to the very varied influences which were brought to bear on its beginnings and development. Had English sculpture of the twelfth century been as purely Norman in origin as the architecture which it accompanied, it must have been as meagre a growth as the corresponding art in Normandy, which only by slow degrees and by late borrowings from southern France at length emerged from a barbaric state. That such native Norman sculpture was indeed introduced into England is shown by the crude figures on the capitals of Durham Castle chapel (1072) and elsewhere. In England, however, at the time of the Conquest, there existed a strong and even virile native tradition going back to the great period of Anglian sculpture in the seventh and eighth centuries and affected more or less profoundly by Scandinavian and Ottonian influences at a later date. Unlike Anglo-Saxon architecture, this school (or schools) of sculpture was not immediately, nor indeed ultimately, overwhelmed by Norman methods; thus any work above the Norman level

Simplify

produced in England for the three generations or so after the Conquest may reasonably be assigned to this earlier tradition. The correctness of this theory is borne out by the fact that sculpture of the superior English types is confined to the small and unimportant churches, and is conspicuous by its absence from the great cathedrals and abbey churches where the Norman tradition was necessarily supreme.

Of works in this English tradition it seems possible to distinguish three distinct types in which respectively the Anglian, the Scandinavian, and the Ottonian influences predominate. In all of these the finer examples must obviously be placed before the Conquest, as after that event they can have lingered on only as rural arts, without the aristocratic or ecclesiastical backing which then at any rate was necessary for the full life of any art. In the late pre-Conquest period the Anglian tradition (Pl. 36 a) was represented by the sculpture of the Winchester school, of which the Romsey rood is the supreme example; the much damaged Crucifixions at Breamore and Headbourne Worthy and the panel at Stepney belong to the same group. After the Conquest a group of tympana, of a purely sculptural type, such as Little Barrington and Tredington (Glos.), may be fairly considered as carrying on the same tradition.

The Scandinavian type is distinguished by a very low relief and, in its earlier examples, by the accompaniment of foliage based upon that of the early eleventh-century Ringerike style. The carved lintel at Southwell, with St. Michael and the Dragon, must almost certainly be assigned to the period before the Conquest, as it is reused material in the early twelfth-century church. To the same period seems also to belong the tympanum at Hoveringham (Notts.) and that with a swine and a Saxon inscription at St. Nicholas, Ipswich. The series is continued after the Conquest in such works as the tympana at Moreton Valence (Glos.) and Fordington (Dorset).

The third influence, the Ottonian, has not hitherto been specifically recognized. It provides, however, the only reasonable explanation of a small but highly important group of sculptures, the date of which has long been in dispute. The strong Byzantine element in the Ottonian revival has long been recognized, and the influence of this revival and the earlier Carolingian tradition on the Winchester school has more than once been pointed out. That Byzantine influence is markedly present in the veiled hands of the Bradford-on-Avon angels, in the draped Crucifix at Langford (Oxon.), and in the throned Madonna and Child at York (Pl. 36 b), is sufficiently obvious, and the Ottonian revival presents itself at the right period and with the necessary connexions to explain its presence in tenth- and eleventh-century England. The York Madonna, a relief-carving in the local Tadcaster stone, stands so isolated in the history of English art that its proper place has given rise to much discussion. If, however, it is viewed as an example of the Ottonian revival adopted in England, we venture to think that most of these difficulties will disappear. It has obvious affinities with the ivories and relief sculptures of the Macedonian revival of Greek art, and its direct connexion with this art by way of Germany is, we think, nearly established by the use in the inscription of the curious looped A. This form of the capital is not uncommon on Ottonian ivories and manuscripts, while it is markedly and almost universally absent from the contemporary work of France. It is furthermore hardly to be found in any work of the twelfth century, and this with the use of the square C in the York inscription is an indication of, at latest, eleventh-century date. Furthermore, if this sculpture be indeed a Byzantine-Ottonian work, its closeness to its eastern original must place it near the beginning of the series and consequently late in the tenth or early in the eleventh century.

The purely Norman type of sculpture in England is marked by an almost childish crudity of drawing and an

entire ignorance of anatomy. Seen perhaps first at Durham
Castle, this type is continued in a series of tympana which are
either entirely barbarous, as at Little Paxton (Hunts.), or as
widely sundered from realism as the odd little figures of the
Magi at Bishop's Teignton (Devon). Even in such accomplished and highly decorative work as the Prior's door at Ely
(Pl. 37 a) the same incapacity to render the human figure is
abundantly evident, though here there is evidence of the influence of the far more accomplished art of southern France.

This southern French influence is the last to make itself felt
in English Romanesque sculpture. It is definitely apparent in
the carved capitals of the crypt at Canterbury, where the
neighbourhood of the Channel ports makes its early appearance probable. The carving of these capitals perhaps dates
from about 1140, but the finest example of this Anglo-French
work appears some twenty years later in the great west doorway at Rochester. Though not challenging comparison with
the great portals of S. Denis, Chartres, and Le Mans, it is
obviously derived directly from them, as is proved by the
presence of the typical jamb-statues of Solomon and the
Queen of Sheba, which here, alone in England, make their
appearance.

SCOTLAND

It is a pity that so little is left to us of the earliest Romanesque architecture of Scotland, for the few relics which do
survive show a blend of native and foreign traditions which
is highly remarkable and instructive. The marriage of Malcolm Canmore to the English Princess Margaret in 1070 may
be considered as marking the first occasion for the introduction of anything Romanesque into the primitive Celtic architecture of the country. The Anglo-Saxon connexion established by this marriage was further strengthened by the
settlement of the English refugees displaced by the Norman
Conquest. The foundations of the chapel built by Malcolm
and his queen at Dunfermline (1072) have been uncovered

and would seem to show that as yet the simple Celtic nave and chancel church was still in use. In the early part of the twelfth century, however, a distinct advance is observable, but it is curious to note that the form of Romanesque in use is based upon the pre-Conquest traditions of northern England, and only betrays the Anglo-Norman in its mouldings and details. The most prominent example of this is in the church of St. Rule, St. Andrews, built about 1125–30, and which Dr. Bilson[1] has shown is closely akin to certain churches in the Saxon tradition on the Yorkshire wolds. The most noticeable feature at St. Rule's is the small but lofty tower of Anglo-Saxon type, which is represented in another example at Restennet Priory.

Side by side with this hybrid art there still survived the Celtic tradition exemplified in the round tower at Abernethy, where the upper windows are distinctively Romanesque.

The full Romanesque style seems hardly to have established itself much before the middle of the twelfth century. The precise date of the existing nave at Dunfermline is unknown, but it is evidently inspired in many of its details by the cathedral of Durham. The earliest work of Jedburgh dates probably from after 1147, when it became an abbey. This work is confined to the choir and has the curious use of the cylindrical pier carried up, through the main arcade, to support the arch of the triforium, which is to be seen at Romsey Abbey in Hampshire.

The only other great Scottish church of the full Romanesque period is the cathedral of Kirkwall, which belongs rather to the history of Norwegian art, as the Orkneys at that time formed part of the Scandinavian kingdom.

A word, however, must be said of the abbey of Kelso, though the surviving portion belongs to the last quarter of the twelfth century. This structure formed the west end of the building and consisted of a transept with arms north and south

[1] *Arch.* lxxii. 55.

of the tower, and a third arm of equal height and dimensions extending to the west of the tower. The body of the church was aisled, and the fortunate survival of an early sixteenth-century description of the building before the destruction of its eastern part shows that precisely the same planning was repeated at the east end also. This highly unusual arrangement no doubt owes its pair of axial towers to a remote Anglo-Saxon influence, but the general plan shows a closer connexion with the east and west choirs of some of the great Romanesque churches of the Rhineland, or with such a church as Nivelles in Belgium. This type of church is in succession from the Carolingian and Ottonian builders, but whether it reached Scotland direct from Germany or through the channel of the English version of the Carolingian style it is now impossible to say.

That some of the Scottish Romanesque buildings were elaborately ornamented is indicated by the little village churches of Dalmeny and Leuchars, but the ornament of the age throughout the country seems directly copied from Anglo-Norman originals and need not be further particularized.

IRELAND

The term Irish Romanesque can most properly be applied to examples of Irish architecture dating from the beginning of the twelfth century to the English conquest in 1170. Though of very minor importance in the general study of the subject, it is nevertheless of considerable interest as an example of a remote and local adaptation of Romanesque forms, combined with features which are of purely native origin.

In general the churches of this age differ little in size, form, and structure from those of the immediately preceding period. That is to say, they follow the simple plan of a rectangular chancel and nave and are only assignable to the twelfth century by reason of their mouldings or decoration. Few of these structures are definitely dated, but fortunately

one of the most important—Cormac's chapel at Cashel—can
be assigned with some certainty to the year 1134. This remarkable little building, founded by the prince-bishop Cormac MacCarthy, King of Desmond, displays features which
must be of the most varied origin. The two slender towers
which flank the east end of the nave have been thought to
show affinities with German Romanesque; it may be, however, that they were inspired by the pair of eastern towers at
Hereford Cathedral, begun some twenty years earlier. The
nave, with its barrel-vault, upper story, and high-pitched stone
roof is evidently of Irish origin, though the presence of ribs to
the vault again shows a foreign and perhaps French influence.
The ribbed quadripartite vault of the chancel must certainly
be due to Anglo-Norman inspiration, as outside this school
and that of Lombardy it would rank as a fairly early example.

Of much simpler form and structure, but almost equally
closely dated, is the church of St. Saviour, Glendalough,
founded, in all probability, by St. Laurence O'Toole before
his elevation to the see of Dublin in 1162. It displays the
scalloped capitals and chevron-ornament of this age, but the
small chancel had the simple barrel-vault of rubble in the
Irish tradition. The partial rebuilding of the cathedral at
Glendalough belongs to an even later period and must be
nearly contemporary with the English conquest; there are
remains of work of the same age also in the Priest's House
and St. Mary's Church. Perhaps the most elaborately enriched building of the age, still in part surviving, is the cathedral of Tuam, where the chancel-arch has five recessed orders
with chevron and other enrichment. A notable feature of
Irish Romanesque is the pedimented doorway of which there
are numerous examples often richly ornamented. Such are
the doorways at Clonfert Cathedral, at Cormac's Chapel, and
at Roscrea. The pediments are commonly much steeper in
pitch than is usual in Anglo-Norman work and partake rather
of the proportions of the Anglo-Saxon triangular head.

The decoration of these buildings combines with the familiar ornaments of Anglo-Norman Romanesque—the chevron, lozenge, meander, etc., a series of motives which are derived directly from the earlier Irish decorative art of the standing-crosses and manuscripts. Even in the rendering of the familiar chevron-ornament, however, there is evidence of a local peculiarity, and often, as at Killeshin (Leix), the lines of the pattern are merely etched on the surface of the stone and accentuated by a delicate beading. Of the native ornaments, perhaps the most striking is the use of human heads on the angles of a capital or order, with the hair carried back into elaborate interlacements of purely Celtic form, again well exemplified at Killeshin. Interlacement itself is very freely used and with it occasionally some form or other of the traditional ribbon-beast is introduced. Figure-sculpture is sparingly used on buildings, but there are a few carved tympana (e.g. Cormac's Chapel, Priest's House, Glendalough, etc.), and an occasional use of single figures under arcading, as at Ardmore. The erection of standing-crosses in the old tradition was still continued in the twelfth century, as is shown by such examples as the cross at Tuam, and the presence of twelfth-century ornament on some of the round-towers or belfries, such as Kildare, shows that this early structural form had not then become obsolete. The introduction of the Cistercian order into Ireland by St. Malachy in 1142 brought Ireland more definitely into touch with continental architectural ideas, and for the first time churches were erected on the continental scale. Even these Irish Cistercian buildings, however, retain traces of native decoration, and the treatment of Romanesque forms at Jerpoint and Baltinglass is local in its inspiration. The English conquest is marked by the rebuilding of Christchurch Cathedral, Dublin, where the ordinary forms of late English Romanesque are for the first time encountered without native admixture.

A survey of Irish architectural decoration, as part of the

general history of Irish sculpture, has recently been published,[1] and for the first time this extremely interesting by-way of Romanesque has been adequately illustrated. The author has found what is certainly a very close resemblance between the detail of the chancel-arch at Rahan and that of the Armenian palace-chapel at Ani, and, on the strength of this, dates the Irish example to the middle of the eighth century. This, we think, is quite at variance with all probability, unless we may suppose that an Irish mason made sketches of Armenian buildings or that an Armenian mason worked in Ireland; the presence of an Armenian bishop (cited by the author) in the neighbourhood does not strengthen the argument. The attempt, in the same work, to antedate the familiar chevron-ornament in Ireland by a century or two must also fail when supported only by earlier examples of simple zigzag decoration in other media, such as has appeared sporadically at almost every date and in almost every art.

SUMMARY BIBLIOGRAPHY

ARCHITECTURE.

Congrès archéologique de France, Caęn, 1908; Rouen, 1926.

G. Huard, *L'Art en Normandie*, 1928.

A. Clapham, *Romanesque Architecture in England after the Conquest*, 1934.

J. Bilson, 'Durham Cathedral and the chronology of its vaults', *Arch. Journ.*, lxxix, 1922.

J. Macgibbon and T. Ross, *Ecclesiastical Architecture of Scotland*, 1896–7.

A. C. Champneys, *Irish Ecclesiastical Architecture*, 1910.

SCULPTURE.

E. S. Prior and A. Gardner, *English Mediaeval Figure-sculpture*, 1913.

F. Henry, *La Sculpture irlandaise*, 1933.

[1] F. Henry, *La Sculpture irlandaise*, 1933.

BRITISH
ISLES

Miles

0   25   50   75   100 125

Kirkwall

Restennet

Leuchars
St. Andrews
Dumfermline
Dalmeny
Edinburgh
Kelso
Jedburgh
Lindisfarne

Carlisle
Durham

York

Tuam
Clonfert
Rahan
Kildare
Roscrea
Dublin
Killishin
Glendalough
Cashel

Blyth
Lincoln
Southwell
Hoveringham
Chester
Binham
N.Elmham
Norwich
Barnack
Peterborough
Brixworth
Ramsey
Worcester
Northampton
Earls Barton
Ely
Leominster
Bury St.Edmunds
Shobdon
Evesham
Clapham
Cambridge
Ipswich
Hereford
Deerhurst
Kilpeck
Tewkesbury
Wing
St.Albans
Colchester
Gloucester
Oxford
Moreton V.
Waltham
Chepstow
Langford
LONDON
Rochester
Reculver
Malmesbury
Westminster
Canterbury
Bath
Romsey
Battle
Dover
Sarum
Winchester
Breamore
Exeter
Fordington
Chichester
Bosham
Christchurch

Ardmore

Chapter VIII

GERMANY

ROMANESQUE architecture in Germany may be divided into three main districts, which though influencing and reacting the one on the other, yet preserve in the earlier part of the period a considerable degree of individuality. These three districts are the Lower Rhine, Saxony in its ancient and widest sense, and southern Germany, including Swabia, Bavaria, and Austria.

The Lower Rhine was the stronghold of Carolingian tradition as befits the chief seat of the first and greatest of the German dynasties. Saxony flourished under the second great dynasty, and was the homeland of Henry the Fowler and Otto the Great, but after the passing of the Saxon house appears to have languished for a period. Southern Germany may be identified with the Salic and the Swabian houses, and within it the district of the Upper Rhine has many distinctive features of its own which perhaps entitle it to form a fourth district.

Throughout most of the country and throughout most of the period there was a continuous conflict between the underlying Carolingian tradition and the strong and steady infiltration of Italian or Lombard art. The eventual amalgamation of these two forces has produced the extemely impressive and varied outline of the Rhineland churches, which for external mass and grouping have hardly been surpassed or even equalled elsewhere. In spite, however, of this monumental character, German Romanesque was constructionally extremely backward and unambitious. It showed itself, in general, singularly impervious to the ideas of the far more advanced French schools, and continued to erect vast churches throughout the twelfth century, and even into the thirteenth century which show no further advance towards the Gothic system than those of the eleventh century. Even the influence of Cluny, transmitted through Hirsau, or that of the Cistercians was largely unavailing in introducing any advance in vault-construction or in causing the general abandonment of the timber-roofed church. The pointed arch and the ribbed vault make a far later appearance in Germany than in any other great European district, and the forms and ornaments of Romanesque linger on almost as belatedly as they do in Italy and Spain.

It will be as well to trace the course of the main component currents of German Romanesque before considering the more distinctive features of the various provinces; these currents run throughout the country, though their expression is unequally marked in the different districts.

The general features of the Carolingian plan have already been touched upon and many of these features are retained unaltered through the Romanesque period. Most noticeable of these is the retention of the west choir which differentiates, so markedly, many of the greatest German churches from those of the rest of Europe. This feature, generally called either the Nuns' Choir or the Winter Choir, is conveniently accommodated in the traditional double-apse plan, but is by no means confined to it, being sometimes set in a square west end and sometimes raised on a gallery over the western entrance. The western choir was also often provided with a crypt, and several German churches are thus provided with two of these features at the two extremities of the building. Outside Germany the west choir is to be found in three French cathedrals—Verdun, Besançon, and Nevers—all no doubt preserving the earlier Carolingian arrangement. The second distinctively Carolingian survival in German Romanesque is the staged tower over the crossing. In the earlier period there seems good reason to suppose that these structures were commonly of timber built in receding and arcaded stages; in the Romanesque period, however, they were constructed in stone and tended to lose some of their original form, which was, however, retained in its entirety in a few corresponding structures of northern Italy (e.g. Chiaravalle by Milan). The circular Carolingian staircase towers were also retained in German Romanesque, accompanied by and forming part of the highly elaborate tower-system which was distinctive of the period. The simple Carolingian type of interior was also retained almost universally, with the main arcade separated from the perfectly plain clerestory, by a large extent of blank wall-surface which served as a field for painted decoration.

Turning now to the intruding element, the Lombard style, we have already seen that the decorative features of the first Romanesque had already penetrated into southern Germany by the early part of the eleventh century, if not by the end of the tenth. Lombard bands and blind arcading are to be seen on the western extension of Trier Cathedral, built between 1016 and 1078, and on the two round west towers of Worms Cathedral of the first half of the same century. The full Lombard style did not penetrate into Germany until the twelfth century; its most distinctive features are the arcaded gallery round the apse and the square Lombard tower, for the Lombard arcaded gable carried across both nave and aisles hardly, if at all, gained a footing in Germany. Marcel Aubert considers that the earliest German example of the arcaded gallery is that at Schwartzrheindorf c. 1150, but it appears as far north as Lund Cathedral in Sweden as early as about 1130, so that it must certainly have been known in Germany before this date. A master-mason from Como built S. Magnus Church in Regensburg in 1139, and Donatus the architect of Lund was also an Italian.

Lastly we find a third introduction into Germany, this time from France, which while leaving the structure and decoration of German churches unaffected, profoundly altered the plan and was largely responsible for the general abandonment of the west choir after the middle of the twelfth century. This was the so-called Hirsau school. The abbey of Hirsau in Franconia (north-west Würtemberg) was the head of the great reform of German Benedictine houses, based on that of Cluny, and the churches of the Hirsau school form a strongly marked type in which practically none of the old Carolingian features are apparent. There are remains of two churches at Hirsau (Fig. 52),[1] the earliest, S. Aurelius, consecrated in 1071, and the second, SS. Peter and Paul, built after the Cluniac reform and consecrated in 1091. Certain alterations to the earlier church brought it into line with the new type, and it is the church of S. Aurelius so altered that formed the model for a large number of subsequent churches in Germany. The excavations now in progress on the site of the second church of Cluny (consecrated 981) seem likely to prove that this church was the original of the Hirsau type. As finally established this consisted of a cruciform church with a short aisled presbytery, apsidal chapels to the transepts, and an aisled nave terminating in two western towers with a porch or narthex between them. Some 130 German convents were reformed under Abbot William of Hirsau, and the building ideas of the order extended beyond it to Benedictine houses such as U. L. F. Halberstadt and Königslutter, Augustinian houses as Hamersleben, and Premonstratensian as Jerichow, Windberg, and Germerode.

Vaulting. Vaulting was confined in the earlier churches in Germany as elsewhere to the apses and crypts, except in certain forebuildings, the minster at Aachen, etc. The vaulting of the side aisles of a normal church first appears in the course of the eleventh century, and the church of S. Aurelius at Hirsau (1055–71) is an early example. The great majority of these vaults are of simple groined form, but an example of the barrel form is to be found in the crypt of S. Wipert, Quedlinburg (*c*. 930). With the completion or rebuilding of the

---

[1] A. Mettler, *Hirsau*, 1928.

two cathedrals of Speyer and Mainz by Henry IV (1056–
1106) we come to a new epoch. Speyer is the earlier and
work was renewed there about 1080; the eastern part of the
nave (the rest is modern) is roofed with a groined and domed
vault over the double bay which may either be placed (as in
the older German view) about 1100, or as Herr Dehio and
M. Aubert[1] think, after the fire of 1137. The system at Speyer
is somewhat similar to that at Mainz (Pl. 41 b), the reconstruction of which was begun under Henry IV, though not
far advanced at his death in 1106; the original roofing with
groined vaults over a double bay, of which remains still exist,
was set up by Archbishop Adalbert (1118–37). Taking into
account the similarity of the two structures, there seems some
reason to suppose that the groined vault at Speyer was at any
rate contemplated from the outset, and that both buildings
were so designed by the end of the eleventh century. The
actual vault at Speyer, however, must be contemporary with
the open arcaded gallery below the level of the eaves, and this
can hardly be placed before about 1120–30. A third example at
Maria Laach was begun early in the twelfth century (founded
1093), and here the choir has a domed groined vault; the
vaulting, however, is on the single-bay system. These three
churches remained without immediate imitators, and perhaps
the next example is the Premonstratensian abbey of Kneksteden founded in 1134, the church of which was finished
under Abbot Hermann (1150–81); here a return is made to
the double bays.

The ribbed vault of the purely Lombard type makes an
appearance in the cathedral of Chur (Switzerland) about
1170–8, but hardly penetrated farther north. Ribbed vaulting on the French system is to be found at the end of the

---

[1] *Congrès arch. de France, Rhénanie*, 1922, p. 224. The comparative
thickness of the walls of Speyer and Mainz, called attention to here, seems
of no great import, as the thinner walls of Speyer are those of wall-recesses
only, which have no structural significance.

twelfth century at Trier and Worms, and from thence onwards it becomes increasingly common, but was only generally adopted towards the middle of the thirteenth century.

LOWER RHINE

The district of the Lower Rhine, which includes also the
valleys of the Mosel and the Main (anciently Lorraine and
Franconia), was the early ecclesiastical centre of Germany.
The three archbishop-electors of the Empire had their sees at
Cologne, Mainz, and Trier, and all three cities had at the base
of their traditions the stable foundation of Roman culture,
and the standing example of Roman structures. The steady-
ing effect of this, as it might seem, remote and half-obliterated
influence, is to be remarked here as elsewhere throughout the
Roman world, for the building tradition in the Rhineland is
more permanent and pronounced than elsewhere in Germany, and only here had new influences from without to con-
tend with a long established and deep-rooted tradition.

In addition to the three great centres mentioned above,
the Salic dynasty added another in the cathedral of Speyer,
which for long remained the burial place of the emperors,
and the lesser cathedrals of Worms and Würzburg were minor
centres of importance.

Besides the cathedrals the district is rich in lesser Romanesque churches of the highest interest and value. Such are
the churches of Cologne, Bonn Minster, S. Kastor, Koblenz,
Maastricht, and the abbeys of Maria Laach, Brauweiler, and
Kneksteden. Transitional churches may also be studied at
Andernach, Limburg a. d. Lahn, and in the Cistercian abbey
of Heisterbach.

The Rhineland was at once the most conservative and the
most advanced of the German districts, clinging to earlier
Carolingian forms clothed in Lombard guise and here and
there experimenting in new forms and types of construction.
The churches in general astonish by their scale, and their

massive grandeur forms no bad expression of the spirit of the Holy Roman Empire.

Plan. The most distinctive feature of the planning of the Rhineland churches of the eleventh and twelfth centuries is the general retention in the larger examples of the Carolingian double-apse plan. Few of the buildings are of a single period or campaign of construction, but throughout every alteration or partial reconstruction the essential balance of the east and west apsidal ends and choirs has been preserved. With the double-apse plan sometimes goes the double-transept plan, and the eastern transept is by no means always more important architecturally than the western. At Mainz, for example, the western transept and choir is far more prominent. On the other hand, the western transept at Maria Laach is unimportant, while at Worms it is omitted altogether. The foundation of the new cathedral at Speyer about 1030 by Conrad II marks a new departure, for though rebuilt by Henry IV *c.* 1082–1106, the present cathedral seems to rest on the earlier foundations. The church is cruciform, but the western choir and apse is abandoned and the west transept reduced to the role of a narthex. Somewhat similar, but with a square east end, was Poppo von Stablo's church at Limburg a. d. Hardt.

The square atrium of the Carolingian builders also persisted uninterruptedly, though becoming more and more occasional as time went on. An eleventh-century example survives at Essen Minster, and another of the first half of the twelfth century at Maria Laach (Fig. 48). The last place is remarkable as possessing a homogeneous building of 1113–56 preserving all the traditional features of the Rhineland both in form and plan.

Throughout the twelfth century even the largest churches had no aisles to the choir.[1] The influence of Hirsau (with its

[1] S. Maria im Kapitol, Cologne, is a special type and as such will be considered later.

aisled choir) was little operative in the district, and it was not until French influence made itself belatedly felt that aisled choirs with ambulatories were introduced, such as Limburg a. d. Lahn (dedicated 1235) and Heisterbach Abbey (Cistercian early thirteenth century).

Internal Elevation. Though the groined vault over the double bay or later the ribbed vault over the same area is occasionally used in Rhineland Romanesque, the use of the alternating pier and column (Stützenwechsel) is highly unusual in the district, one of the few examples being at Kneksteden. There is, however, a group of such churches in old Lorraine which includes those of Echternach (before 1031) and Susteren, and another and later group in Alsace. Normally there is no vertical division into bays except where it has been added for a later vault-system. In the cathedral of Speyer, however, the intermediate pier carries a pair of wall-arches which enclose the clerestory windows. A somewhat similar arrangement is employed at Worms and Mainz, though at the latter place the arches are turned below the clerestory. The piers generally throughout the district are of simple rectangular plan and the arches are unmoulded. S. Ursula, Cologne (after 1106?), is unusual in the district in having a three-storied structure, with a fully developed triforium.

Tower-System. The full complement of towers of a great Rhineland church was six, including two main towers or lanterns over the east and west crossings, where the west transept existed, or with the second main tower over the west end of the church. The subsidiary towers were commonly used for staircases and were generally of the round form of Carolingian tradition or square in the later Italian fashion. The complete arrangement may be seen at the cathedrals of Worms (Pl. 38 a), Speyer, and Mainz, and at the abbey of Maria Laach. In all these the main lanterns take the octagonal form, while the subsidiary towers are placed in the re-entrant angles of the transept or nave, or, as at Mainz and Laach (Pl. 38 b), they are set axially and tangent at the ends of the transept. At Speyer, where the western apse is abandoned, the lantern at this end has been restored over the middle of the 'Kaiser-Halle' or narthex which forms a western transept. At Brauweiler Abbey (near Cologne) the western lantern is replaced by a massive square tower after the Westphalian fashion. The lanterns are normally enriched with external arcaded galleries, reminiscent of their Carolingian prototypes, while the staircase towers are divided into numerous stages enriched with Lombard bands and blind-arcading.

A less elaborate system of towers may be seen at S. Kastor, Koblenz, where there are two square towers on the west front and a second pair flanking the east apse. At Bonn Minster there are two towers flanking the apse and a high octagonal tower over the crossing.

A common method of covering the square towers is the so-called helm-roof. It consists in carrying up the four walls into high gables, from the apex of which ridges run up to meet at the point of the spire, the intervening planes running down to the angles of the tower. It is thus a square pyramidal roof set diagonally on the tower. Many of the existing examples are modern restorations, but early engravings prove how frequently this form of roof was used throughout this and many of the other German provinces. The form is exactly reproduced in the well-known Anglo-Saxon tower at Sompting (Sussex).

NORTH GERMANY

The two chief districts of North Germany for Romanesque building are those of Westphalia and Saxony. They include a considerable number of early churches mainly connected with the Saxon dynasty, with Bernward of Hildesheim, Meinwerk of Paderborn, and other bishops of the eleventh century.

Plan. Though not so frequent as in the Rhine district, the double-apse plan occurs fairly often in the north, as for example at Gernrode, S. Michael, Hildesheim, Münster, and Naumberg Cathedrals. The more usual type, however, is the cruciform plan with an aisleless eastern arm and apsidal chapels on the east of the transept. Numerous churches of this type survive in Saxony, and it is the one adopted in Franconia at Hersfeld Abbey (an earlier building (Fig. 12) altered *c.* 1040), which was closely copied at Würzburg Cathedral ((Fig. 49) about the same period). With the advent of the Hirsau reform the normal Saxon plan required only the addition of aisles to the presbytery to bring it into line with the new ideas. The finest example of the Hirsau type is the ruined church at Paulinzelle (Pl. 40 *a*, and Fig. 54), Thuringia (1105–19), which has the large Cluniac narthex in addition. The Hirsau school brought with it also the column-basilica which became frequent in north Germany in the later part of the twelfth century.

The most frequent early arrangement of supports in Saxony is the alternating pier and column, which is indeed the most distinctive feature of the district. Perhaps the earliest example is at Gernrode Abbey (Fig. 50), which seems largely to preserve the plan of the tenth century, though the superstructure is mainly of the twelfth century. Here the alternation is simple, forming a double bay, but elsewhere, particularly at Hildesheim, the ordinary arrangement is the alternation of one pier with two columns. This arrangement may be seen at the Cathedral, S. Michael (Pl. 41 *a* and Fig. 47) and S. Godehard, Hildesheim, Münster, Goslar, Quedlinburg, and Frose. Unlike the early examples in Italy, which were so arranged to support a series of diaphragm-arches, there seems to have been not the slightest intention in Saxony to apply the alternating pier to any system of roof-support, for it was not until the end of the twelfth century that stone-vaulting was generally adopted in Saxony even in the aisles. The alternation of two columns and one pier must thus have been adopted either for effect or by copying some older building. In point of fact a somewhat similar arrangement was employed in the church of S. Demetrius, Salonica (late fifth century), and in the seventh-century restoration of the church of the Holy Sepulchre, either of which may have inspired the scheme.

Gernrode Abbey is also notable as being the earliest example in the district of the three-storied building, for the nave here has a fully developed triforium with six arches grouped in pairs to each double bay. The system, however, was never popular in Germany until the latter part of the Romanesque period, though an important example of four internal storeys survives in the nave of the cathedral of Tournai (1171).

Tower-System. The tower-system in north Germany is much less elaborate than is usual in the Rhineland. The commonest form is the pair of towers flanking the western front, but occasionally, as in the eleventh-century cathedral of Meissen or at Göllingen Abbey, a pair of towers was set in the west angles of the transept and nave, while at Naumburg Cathedral there were two pairs of towers flanking the east and west apses. Two systems, however, are distinctive of this part of the country, the one appertaining rather to Westphalia and the other to Saxony. The Westphalian type is the extremely massive west tower, forming a solid frontispiece to the building and sometimes flanked by subsidiary staircase towers. This is a Carolingian arrangement first exemplified in the forebuilding of the minster at Aachen. The single tower may be seen at S. Patroklus, Soest (early thirteenth century), while the tower flanked by round staircase towers is well exemplified at Paderborn Cathedral (twelfth century) and Frekenhorst (Pl. 39 a) (early twelfth century). The Saxon type is a special treatment of the pair of western towers by the provision of a high gallery connecting them above the main roof of the church and often added to an earlier building. This gallery is sometimes of two stories and even develops into a solid mass of building extending completely across the west front. The most notable examples of this gallery are at Gernrode Abbey (late eleventh century), Korvey Abbey (Pl. 39 b) (twelfth century), and Goslar Neuwerkkirche (late twelfth century).

SOUTH GERMANY

The South German school covers a vast extent of territory, extending from Alsace to Austria, and including Switzerland, Alamannia, and Bavaria. The Upper Rhine with Alsace and Switzerland form a fairly marked subdivision, while Bavaria with its early centres at Regensburg, Augsburg, and Salzburg provided models for the south-eastern marks of the Empire.

Plan. The early churches of Bavaria showed a marked preference for the simple basilican type of church, perhaps due to their being the nearest and most open to Italian influence. Of this simple type, with column or pier arcades extending from end to end of the building, are the Niedermunster and S. Jakob, Regensburg (Fig. 53), Freising Cathedral, and Moosburg. A variant having a west transept only was adopted at Augsburg Cathedral, the early Cathedral and S. Emmeran, Regensburg, and S. Jakob, Bamberg, all early in the eleventh century. The ordinary cruciform plan was introduced in certain churches of the Hirsau type, of which Prüfening with its Byzantine wall-paintings is the most important.

In the Upper Rhine district a few early churches (such as Strasbourg Cathedral) adopted the ancient T-cross plan, and throughout Alamannia there are numerous churches displaying the square east end in place of the apse.

Internal Elevation. The general type of the south German churches is of the simplest description. The supports are indifferently either square piers (Pl. 40 b), as at Reichenau, Freising, and Prüfening, or columns, as at Constance, Alpirsbach, Schwarzach, Augsburg, and S. Jakob, Regensburg. The alternate system is very infrequent except in the late Romanesque churches of Alsace. The superstructure is commonly of the simplest form, without a triforium story and with a clerestory of plain round-headed windows. The eleventh- and twelfth-century churches are commonly timber-roofed, at any rate in their main spans, and it is only at the end of the century that this system gave way to stone-vaulted churches in Alsace.

Towers and *Exterior*. The towers are often in pairs and flank one end or the other of the church. An eleventh-century staircase tower of the plainest description still survives at Regensburg Cathedral. Pairs of towers flanking the choir still stand at Eichstätt Cathedral, Prüfening, Ellwangen, Altenstadt bei Schongau, and elsewhere, which are more or less close copies of Lombard towers such as those of S. Abbondio, Como. The German examples are, however, commonly covered by a pyramidal or helm roof.

The external treatment of the apses, &c., is often very Italian in character, as, for example, the arcaded apses of Gurk Cathedral, the Lombard bands and cornice arcading of All Saints Chapel, Regensburg, and the west front and apse of Rosheim in Alsace.

CENTRALLY-PLANNED CHURCHES

Centrally-planned churches have a long history and played an important part in German architecture. Their form is extremely varied, ranging from the oval and round to the square and cruciform. The prevailing type, however, is based rather on the minster at Aachen than, as elsewhere, on the church of the Holy Sepulchre at Jerusalem, and the minster at Aachen had an influence far beyond the confines of Germany. The church of the Holy Sepulchre, however, served as a model for the still-existing rotunda at Constance[1] (late tenth century) and no doubt for other churches of the same type.

The earliest of the centrally-planned churches in Germany seems to have partly survived in the nave (Fig. 2) of S. Gereon at Cologne, a church commemorating the martyrs of the Theban legion, mentioned as existing by Gregory of Tours in 590. The plan, an oval decagon with semicircular niches in each face, is similar to that of the so-called Temple of Minerva Medica at Rome (c. 260).[2] A similar but smaller chapel on the Festamarienburg at Würzburg is said to have been built in 706, but the superstructure is of later date.

The palace chapel of Charles the Great at Aachen (795–805) has already been dealt with. It was copied during the same period at the palace at Nijmwegen[3] (Holland) and Thionville, and in 982 at S. Jean at Liége (Belgium). The internal elevation was copied in the west choir of Essen Collegiate church (end of the tenth century) and in the west tribune of S. Maria im Kapitol at Cologne. The series of round and polygonal churches includes also S. Michael's, Fulda, a cemetery-chapel of 818–22 with a crypt, S. Martin, Bonn (destroyed 1812), Wimpfen im Tal, Drüggelde near Soest, and Ottmarsheim (consecrated 1049). At Wimpfen the earliest building (eleventh century) was twelve-sided with a triple apse to the east and two square staircase towers flanking a forebuilding on the west. An octagonal building of the same nature was built by Conrad II or Henry III (1024–56) on the Georgenberg at Goslar; it had also three apses and two octagonal staircase towers at the west end. An eastern church was added in 1145.

In the twelfth and thirteenth centuries examples of the round church became numerous particularly in eastern

---

[1] Built by Bishop Conrad 'sepulchrum Domini in similitudine illius Jerusolimitani'.

[2] A chapel at Zara (Dalmatia) and the ninth-century church of the Trinity at Spalato, both cemetery-chapels, were on a similar plan.

[3] Reconstructed in the twelfth century.

Bavaria and the former Austrian provinces.[1] Here they commonly served as cemetery-chapels, as at Fulda, and often stood in immediate juxtaposition to a larger church. They are of a simple round plan without internal arcades and are finished with an apsidal or horseshoe chancel and a high pyramidal roof. The crypts which often occur below were no doubt used as bone-holes for the cemetery. Many of these chapels are richly decorated, as for example, Hartberg in Styria and Mödling in Lower Austria.

One of the essential features of the palace and castle-chapels descended from Aachen was the provision of an upper story for the use of the family, while the ground-floor was reserved for retainers and servants. At Aachen itself the upper gallery was formed by the broad tribunes or triforium which surrounded the church and represented the Matroneum of S. Vitale, Ravenna, from which it was copied. Late in the eleventh century the earlier polygonal or circular form of palace-chapel was abandoned in favour of a two-storied square building with four internal columns forming nine equal bays. The central bay of the ground-floor was not roofed, but communicated directly with the upper story and was commonly carried up still higher to form a lantern; the upper floor thus formed a gallery round a square central well. These 'double-chapels' (*Doppel-Capellen*) were evidently of German or more especially Rhineland origin, as their occurrence is very infrequent elsewhere.[2] Examples may be noted at the castles of Nuremberg, Eger (Bohemia), Freiburg a. d.

[1] In Lower Austria eighteen have been noted dating from the twelfth and thirteenth centuries, twelve in Styria, and about the same number in Bohemia. See *Mitteilungen d. K. K. C. C. Baudenkmale*, iii. 263 (Lower Austria), and iv. 47 (Styria); xvi. 180 (Bohemia). Dehio and von Bezold estimate that there were over 100 in Bavaria, the Austrian provinces, and Bohemia.

[2] e.g. Chapels of the Bishops' Palaces at Laon (France) and Hereford, and at Ledöje (Denmark), &c. That at Hereford was built by a bishop from Lorraine, and is, singularly enough, the earliest surviving example to which a definite date can be assigned (1079–95).

Unstrut, and Landsberg, in the archbishop's palace at Mainz, and on a more elaborate plan at Schwartzrheindorf.

Another type of central plan consists of a central square building with apses or square-ended wings projecting from three or four faces. The chapel of S. George at Regensburg is an example with apses, and Weisskirchen (Bohemia) has the square-ended projections.

The Trefoil Plan. This type of church, which consists of a nave, with or without aisles, and a crossing from which project three apses, makes a curiously early appearance in Germany in the isolated and elaborate example at S. Maria im Kapitol, Cologne (1065). There can, however, be no doubt that the type came still earlier from north Italy, where the essence of the scheme is present in the sixth-century church of S. Lorenzo Maggiore at Milan. An interesting twelfth-century authority may be cited in support of this conclusion. In a chronicle of the abbey of Rolduc[1] near Maastricht (Holland) it is recorded that a certain monk Embricus built a crypt at Rolduc in the Lombard style (*scemate longobardino*) which was inaugurated in 1108. This crypt which still exists[2] is of the trefoiled form, and it may thus be concluded that at that period the trefoiled plan was definitely regarded as north Italian. S. Maria im Kapitol at Cologne (Fig. 51) was dedicated, as a completely new church, by Archbishop Anno in 1065. Originally its main spans were wooden roofed, the groined vaults being confined to the aisles and ambulatories. The last are carried completely round the apsidal transepts and eastern arm and the whole plan is very closely akin to that of S. Fidele at Como. The Como church was refounded and perhaps rebuilt in 964 (the date of the translation of S. Fidele); the existing church

---

[1] P. J. H. Cuypers, 'Historique de la fondation de l'abbaye de Rolduc', *Rev. de l'art chrétien*, 1892, pp. 16–25, 116–25.

[2] H. A. Diepen in his recent book *Die romanische Bauplastik in Klosterrat* (1930) maintains, however, that the trefoiled feature here dates from a later period of the twelfth century.

seems partly to belong to the eleventh century, but according to Kingsley Porter is a homogeneous building of the twelfth century. It is almost inconceivable, as some have argued, that this church was a copy of that at Cologne, and it is probable that both were based on some earlier model. The church of S. Maria at Cologne remained apparently without imitators for over a century, after which the scheme was extensively revived, and the trefoiled plan, but without the ambulatory, was reproduced at Gross S. Martin, Cologne (after 1185), Holy Apostles, Cologne (after 1199), S. Quirin at Neuss (begun 1209), Roermond (begun 1218), and Bonn (1220).

Crypts. The crypts of German churches are often of considerable size and importance, though they hardly ever reached the extent of some of the English examples. An example of the simplest type survives at Werden a. Ruhr. It is of the ninth century, and consists of a central confessio with an encircling corridor and long approaching corridors similar to the early examples in Italy and England. At Constance Cathedral (995–1018) the corridor has been omitted, and the confessio has become an apartment of three aisles, though still considerably narrower than the presbytery above. The fully developed type follows the plan of the superstructure, but seldom extends beyond the presbytery. Several of the German churches had crypts below both the eastern and western choirs, and the remains of that under the west apse of Henry II's cathedral at Bamberg have recently been excavated. S. Wipert's crypt at Quedlinburg (936) is unusual in having the arcade supporting the vault carried round in apsidal form and thus producing an ambulatory. Perhaps the finest of the later German crypts is that under the presbytery and aisles of Gurk Cathedral, where the superstructure and vault are supported on six main piers and ninety-six columns.

Attention has recently been called[1] to an entirely different

[1] M. R. Maere in *Bull. Mon.* xci (1932), 81.

type of crypt which seems to have taken its rise from certain late Carolingian buildings and to have been extensively employed in later German Romanesque, particularly in the Low Countries. In this type the structure of the crypt is entirely outside and to the east of the main building, and indeed only deserves its name in being sunk partially below the surface of the ground. The earliest of these structures appears to be that added in 836 to the church of S. Philbert de Grandlieu and of which the plan has been recovered by excavation. Others, such as those at S. Emmeran at Regensburg and Werden a. Ruhr, are connected with earlier crypts under the east apse of their respective churches. Others again, following more closely the type at Grandlieu, completely envelop the east end of the church, and of these good examples survive at Susteren (Holland) and Fosse (Belgium). The plan of these structures is extremely varied, the main feature at Korvey having been a cruciform chapel projecting far to the east, that at Regensburg somewhat similar, while those at Grandlieu and its imitators resemble a large extension to the presbytery added to provide a greatly increased altar accommodation. It would seem possible that this unusual arrangement of the crypt may have inspired the builders of Palermo Cathedral, where again the crypt is planned beyond the main east wall of the building.

Ornament. The architectural ornament of the Carolingian churches was based almost entirely on classical models. The use in the greater buildings of actual antique material provided a model for the local craftsmen, and at Aachen, Lorsch, and elsewhere they copied, not unsuccessfully, the details of the Corinthian and Composite orders. The capitals at Lorsch are so good as to lead Lasteyrie to deny the possibility of their eighth- or ninth-century date; they are, however, entirely in place when compared with German work of the same and a succeeding age. In the Ottonian period the capitals are generally of greatly inferior excellence and the foliage becomes distinctly barbaric. Throughout the period there is a curious use of the separate entablature interposed between the capital and the arch springing, which seems to anticipate the classical Renaissance. This is perhaps first seen in the Vorhalle at Korvey (873–85), and is repeated at Paderborn (S. Bartholomew), Hildesheim (S. Michael), and at Essen Minster early in the eleventh century.

The work of Bishop Bernward at S. Michael, Hildesheim (after 1022), provides an early example of the plain cushion-capital in Germany. This form makes so nearly a contemporary appearance in northern Italy that it is difficult to determine which region can claim priority. Once established in Germany its use became nearly universal, and its heavy outline remained unrelieved by subdivision or carving until the middle of the twelfth century. It forms indeed one of the distinctive features of early German Romanesque and emphasizes the massive and somewhat ungainly character of the accompanying architecture. In northern Germany a local variety of the cubical capital was in use in the twelfth century, in which the upright faces instead of being cut to a semi-circular form (as in the cushion-capital) take the form of an inverted triangle; a good example is to be seen in the Premonstratensian abbey of Jerichow.

Towards the middle of the twelfth century carved capitals become fairly common, more especially in the north and in Alsace; they generally preserve the outline of the cushion-form, and when they depart from it are apt to assume a hunched and rather ungainly outline. The great majority of these carved capitals exhibit only foliage ornament, often of great richness and following the Byzantine-Italian type of fennel-acanthus rather than the Roman form more favoured in France, e.g. Hamersleben Abbey, Reichenberg, Gelnhausen Palace, Worms Synagogue. Here and there, however, there are instances of a return to the imitation of the capitals of the classical orders which are somewhat surprising in their

Romanesque setting. Thus there are Corinthian and Ionic capitals in the so-called library at Huysburg Abbey and Composite capitals in the cathedral at Speyer.

In addition to foliage, use is less commonly made of animal and human forms; the former, as at Neuweiler (Sebastian Kapelle) and Reichenberg Crypt, are often direct borrowings from Italy, and the unusual occurrence of historied capitals is commonly to be ascribed to French influence.

Occasionally the shafts of smaller columns are completely covered with a foliage-diaper (Reichenberg, Ilsenburg), and still more occasionally the attic-base is also enriched with carving in addition to the spur-ornament.

The decorative influence of Italy is more apparent, as is reasonable, in southern Germany than elsewhere. The elaborate Schottenthor (Pl. 44) at S. Jakob, Regensburg, borrows much of its decoration from Italy, and such purely southern features as the knotted shaft (Mödling, Austria) and the lion-support to a column or shaft (Königslutter, &c.) make an occasional appearance.

The Anglo-Norman chevron-ornament, though widespread, is also infrequent and only makes its appearance in late Romanesque work.

Sculpture. The beginning of German stone-sculpture is amongst the most obscure periods in the history of Romanesque art. In its early examples it exhibits none of those preliminary attempts which indicate a new-born art, but these scanty survivals seem rather the decadent examples of an art which has passed its prime and become stiff and stereotyped. That the Carolingian and later the Ottonian revival set Germany at the head of Europe in respect to the minor arts is an undoubted fact, but if anything was attempted in the domain of figure-sculpture, the art has disappeared almost without leaving a trace. There is, however, one reasonable and quite satisfactory explanation of this highly remarkable gap, which we have already touched upon in an earlier chapter. This is the prevalence of the use of stucco both for pure decoration and also for figure-subjects on a large scale. The perishable nature of the material in a northern climate is quite sufficient explanation for the disappearance of the majority of such examples as repeated rebuilding might otherwise have suffered to survive, and the occasional but continued use of stucco side by side with stone, to a far later age, makes it extremely probable that these survivals indicate a much more general use in the earlier ages. Such use indeed is fully testified by documents of the Carolingian period.

With this background of stucco modelling it is well to approach the study of the surviving examples of the earliest German stone-sculpture, which thus cease to be the isolated and unaccountable survivals which they would otherwise appear.

To the purely Carolingian tradition, in this material, are perhaps to be assigned the notable stone figures of Christ, S. Emmeran, and S. Dionysius at S. Emmeran, Regensburg, which were made by Abbot Reginward (1048–64). They stand apart from most of the other early German sculptures, and in form and treatment may well be a rendering in stone of a stucco model, while their early date renders any other derivation difficult.

The splendours of the Ottonian revival in painting, miniature, ivory, and metal work may still be studied in libraries and museums in considerable quantity, and at Reichenau Oberzell a whole scheme of painted decoration has been preserved. Much of this art was based on earlier Carolingian traditions, but into this a new element has been introduced in a new and direct contact with Byzantine art as it was revived under the Macedonian dynasty. The effect of the marriage of Otto II with the Greek princess Theophano and the effective regency of this princess for several years after his death may, in many of its applications, have been exaggerated, but that Greek art had a strong if not controlling influence over German figure-sculpture for the next century or more is susceptible of proof. Of the dozen or more examples of sculpture belonging to the eleventh or early twelfth century which are available for general study a good half show definite evidence of direct Byzantine influence. Thus the figures at Gernrode (Pl. 42 a) and Münster are evidently directly copied from reliefs of the Macedonian age, and the same applies to the figure of Plectrudis at Cologne. The Virgin and Child at Liége Museum is again a coarsened copy of a Byzantine relief, as is proved by the Byzantine bolster on the throne, while the figure of St. Peter from Egmond (Holland), now in the Rijks Museum at Amsterdam, abandons all concealment and announces itself in Greek as Hagios Petrus.[1] At Enger in Westphalia is a figure partly of stucco and partly of stone, commemorating a certain Widukind, and here, as though by inadvertence, the hand is given the attitude of the Greek blessing, though the figure is purely secular. All these Greek features are exemplified in contemporary works in ivory or paintings, while the chapel of S. Bartholomew by Bishop Meinwerk (1009–36) at Paderborn[2] is stated definitely in a contemporary life of the bishop to have been erected by Greek workmen, and the character of the building fully bears out the statement.

Amongst the most remarkable of early German sculptures is the great rock relief called the Externstein (Pl. 43), cut by order of Bishop Heinrich von Werl of Paderborn in the Teutoburger Wald and adjoining the grotto-chapel of the Holy Sepulchre there founded in 1117. To the extreme infrequency of such reliefs in Romanesque art must be added the highly unusual treatment of the figures and the remarkable iconography. The subject is the Descent from the Cross,

---

[1] The figure may be compared with one on a lintel of the church of S. Thomas at Strasbourg.

[2] G. Humann, *Die Baukunst unter Bischof Meinwerk von Paderborn*, 1918.

above the left arm of which is represented a sort of astral body or Kaa, with the Resurrection attributes. The figures themselves have a rude vigour and an eastern type of costume, which almost leads one to suppose that some returned crusader had studied the Assyrian sculptures of the Nahr el Kelb during the passage of the army down the Syrian coast.

In southern Germany, or rather Switzerland, two carvings deserve further consideration. The first of these is the Crucifixion at Herznach (Aarau Museum, Switzerland), and the second a carving from the remains of the first minster at Schaffhausen. The former is dated to the time of Bishop Landeolus of Basel, c. 961, and the latter to the date of the church of 1064. In both the one and the other we seem to see affinities with English stone-carving of the later Anglo-Saxon period. Though more crudely rendered the Crucifixion has certain features in common with the Romsey Rood, while the figure at Schaffhausen could be quite closely paralleled by a number of late Anglo-Saxon figures such as those on the tower at Langford (Oxon.). Intercourse between Germany and England during the tenth century was sufficiently close to account for such an interchange of ideas, including as it did the marriage of a sister of Athelstan to the Emperor Otto I. The Greek currents in the Ottonian revival would likewise explain features in late Anglo-Saxon sculpture for which it is otherwise difficult to account. Such, as we have seen, are the angels with the Byzantine veiling of the hands at Bradford-on-Avon and in Ethelwold's Benedictional, and such also is the strongly Byzantine figure of the Virgin and Child at York. The looped A of this inscription appears on an ivory of Otto II and his Empress which is of definitely Byzantine work as its inscription is partly in Greek; it is also to be found on purely Greek work of nearly the same period. The whole question, in any case, is worthy of a full investigation, and it seems probable that many more examples of the German sculpture of this age survive detached from their context and thus unidentified and unillustrated.

Before passing on to later German sculpture a few words must be said on that extraordinary revival of the arts under Bishop Bernward of Hildesheim (993–1022), a revival dismissed in four paragraphs by M. Molinier in Michel's *Histoire de l'art* with the patronizing remark that they are 'works which testify more to good intentions than to ability in design'.[1] One does not expect, it is true, the masterpieces of Romanesque art to be produced at the outset of the eleventh century, but that works of such quality and variety should have been produced at all is, to say the least of it, astonishing. Bishop Bernward was the tutor of the young Emperor Otto III, and according to his biographer his enthusiasm for art was so great that he set up workshops in his own palace at Hildesheim. The metal-work of his own time, which has survived, include the celebrated bronze doors, the great paschal candlestick called the Christ-column (Christus-Säule), and the two small candlesticks found in his grave by Bishop Berno in 1194. Most, if not all of these objects, were provided for the furnishing of Bernward's own abbey of S. Michael, Hildesheim. The bronze doors have recently (1926) received full treatment by Professor Goldschmidt. He draws attention to the remarkable resemblance of the figure-subjects to certain miniatures of Alcuin's Bible in the Bamberg Staatsbibliothek and there can be no doubt that the iconography is based on Carolingian miniatures. The modelling is remarkably good for its age and is of better quality than that of the figures on the rival bronze doors of Augsburg Cathedral, which is perhaps nearly contemporary. The paschal candlestick has spiral figure-reliefs representing twenty-four incidents in the

---

[1] Rivoira, on the other hand, thinks the rendering of the nude on the bronze doors so advanced that it cannot be earlier than the thirteenth century (*Lombardic Architecture*, ii. 310). Both opinions are evidently the result of a purely nationalist point of view.

life of Christ from the Baptism to the Entry into Jerusalem. On the base are four little figures representing the rivers of Paradise and perhaps the earliest examples of spur-ornaments in Romanesque art. The head-types in these reliefs have close resemblances to the Metz group of ivories of late ninth- and early tenth-century date, and Professor Goldschmidt considers that 'the sources of the Bernward art appear to be derived in great part from Lorraine'. The spiral form of the reliefs is of course borrowed from the columns of Trajan and M. Aurelius at Rome or that of Arcadius at Constantinople. The two candlesticks (Bernward Leuchter) are the earliest examples of a series which includes the Gloucester candlestick, and it seems highly probable that the latter is an imported work with an added inscription. They bear the distinctive Romanesque ornament of intertwined men and beasts, though the action here is not so violent as it was later to become. The metal-work of Hildesheim was not without its effect in Germany, and from it may be derived most of the later monumental metal-work of the country. It will be sufficient here to mention the candelabra of Bishop Azelin (1044–54) and Hezilo (1054–79) at Hildesheim Cathedral, the tomb-plate of the anti-king Rudolf of Swabia (*c*. 1080) at Merseberg, the splendid early twelfth-century brazen font at Liége, the early twelfth-century bronze doors of Gnesen Cathedral (Poland) with scenes from the life of S. Adalbert, and at Novgorod, a Saxon work of the middle of the century, and finally the bronze figures of bishops at Magdeburg.

The later bronze doors were copied in wood at S. Maria im Kapitol, Cologne, a work of much disputed date but probably of the latter part of the twelfth century.

Altar-frontals, also of gilt bronze, of the type of that at Aachen (end of tenth century) and that given by Henry II to the cathedral of Basel (*c*. 1020), were the parents of the remarkable collection of twelfth-century works of the same type which still survive in the churches of Denmark.

During the first half of the twelfth century German sculpture, for some reason or other which it is difficult to explain, fell very largely into disuse, and though an attenuated succession of works could be produced to fill the gap, it is only after the middle of the century that any revival of importance is to be noticed. When this does happen we find the art still very largely controlled by the same influences which we have observed in the earlier period. In sculpture as in architecture Germany remained largely unaffected by France until the close of the twelfth century.

Quite in the earlier Byzantine tradition is the west gallery front from Gröningen, near Halberstadt (now in the Kaiser Friedrich Museum), the tympanum of S. Ursula at Cologne, and the Majesty from Petersberg by Fulda. These works may be compared with the stucco-reliefs of the altar-canopy of S. Ambrogio of Milan. In descent from the figure-types of S. Emmeran of Regensburg, we find such works as Bishop Adelog's choir-screen (c. 1186) at S. Michael, Hildesheim, with a series of standing figures under elaborate canopies or the stucco-reliefs from the Liebfrau Kirche, Halberstadt. Perhaps of the same origin, but obviously a very close copy of a classical original, is the well-known bronze lion (1166) of Henry the Lion in the Domplatz at Brunswick.

The revival of north Italian sculpture in the twelfth century also appears to have had some influence in Germany. The very charming Flight into Egypt (Pl. 42 b) in Worms Cathedral, though signed by a German Otto, is closely allied with such Italian carving as that on the pulpit at S. Ambrogio, Milan. The same influence may also be traced in Belgium, not so much in that country itself, but in the exported Tournai marble fonts in England, such as those at Winchester Cathedral and East Meon.

French influence begins to penetrate, as is natural, at first from the south. It may be seen very definitely in the tympanum of Peterhausen by Constance (now at Karlsruhe), *c.* 1170, and in the sculpture of Basel Minster (*c.* 1180–1200). Its later works hardly concern our present purpose, but it is not a little remarkable to find it in direct conjunction with the richest Romanesque setting as in the Marktportal at Mainz Cathedral (end of the twelfth century), the early thirteenth-century golden portal at Freiberg, and the mid-thirteenth-century doorway at S. Stefan's Dom, Vienna. With the sculpture of Magdeburg Cathedral (1210–20) and Bamberg (*c.* 1240) the whole feeling is more definitely Gothic.

HUNGARY

Romanesque architecture in Hungary was in no sense and at no time an independent contribution to the development of the art; a late-comer among the Christian states of Europe, formed of an alien and Asiatic race, its early architecture was of necessity a series of borrowings from its older neighbours. These borrowings, however, form a somewhat remarkable sequence and produced at least two highly individual groups; a study of their origin and expression is thus not without interest and value in a general survey of Romanesque art.

The Magyars' career of raid and rapine was finally cut short in 955 at the battle of Lech by Otto the Great. The conversion of the nation to Christianity was one of the conditions of the peace of 973, but though the then duke Geiza was himself baptized, it was to his son St. Stephen (1001–38) that the actual establishment of the Hungarian Church was due. St. Stephen divided the country into ten dioceses and ordered each group of ten villages to build a church. That these ordinances were carried out is indicated by a decree of the synod of Szabolcs, 1092, that such of these churches as had been destroyed should be rebuilt. Stephen himself built the palatine church of Székesfehérvár (Stuhlweissenburg or Alba regalis), which was to serve as the palace-church and tomb-house. Benedictine monasteries also were founded, the earliest in 999 and others during the eleventh century.

Certain remains of the eleventh- and early twelfth-century cathedrals perhaps still exist, and portions of others have been recovered by excavation, so that from these survivals some idea may be gained of the characteristics of this first building era. The cathedral of Pécs (Fünfkirchen), a building of the eleventh and twelfth centuries,[1] survives largely intact, though it has suffered much from rebuilding and restoration. In general the churches were of the aisled basilican plan with three eastern apses, roofed in timber and with neither triforium nor alternating piers. The cathedral of Pécs (Fig. 55) had a choir raised over a crypt and with a 'pontile' in front. All these features show clearly that the twelfth-century Romanesque of Hungary was an importation from north Italy and reproduced the main features of the Italian churches of the tenth and eleventh centuries. Certain decorative features also indicate sufficiently clearly the same parentage. Three of these churches, however, Székesfehérvár,[2] Esztergom (Gran), and Pécs, are or were provided with four towers set symmetrically in pairs at the east and west ends of the building. Those at Pécs form salients to the main building, but the others are within the main walls. This unusual arrangement, foreign to Italy and not closely paralleled in Germany, has given rise to many theories, of which the latest—that it is derived from the ruined Roman castra of Pannonia and Dacia—is perhaps the least likely of all. The placing of towers both in Italy and Germany is subject to much variation, and it is only necessary to suppose that the architect of one of these Hungarian churches chose this particular disposition and that the others were copied from it. M. Gál ascribes the foundation of these churches to the period 1030–60 and makes Pécs the latest of them. The most remarkable surviving features of their decoration consist of the fragments of the ciborium of the nave-altar at Pécs with

---

[1] It was burnt in 1064 and subsequently restored.
[2] Now destroyed but partly excavated 1862–82.

the sculptured decoration of the staircases leading down into the crypt. M. Gál considers that the ciborium, which consisted of a rectangular chapel level with the nave and having a ribbed vault supporting the high altar above, was erected about 1130–40; it would seem more likely to belong to the second half of the century. Its decoration is almost entirely of north Italian character, and is, in part, of archaic type—interlace, acanthus-diaper, &c.; the vault-ribs, on the other hand, are of the developed moulded form and not square like the earlier ribs of Italy. The staircase-sculptures are perhaps of about the same date and present a remarkable series of reliefs of the Old Testament and the Nativity.

The second phase of Hungarian Romanesque which displays a certain amount of French influence, perhaps began with the introduction of the Cistercian Order in 1142. None of their early churches, however, survive, and it is with the Benedictine abbey of Vértesszenkereszt (founded 1146) and the second cathedral of Kalocsa (second half of the twelfth century) that this influence becomes apparent. It is not very marked in the structure of the abbey church which had a system of groined vaults, but excavations have shown that the cathedral had a developed ambulatory plan with radiating chapels, a transept, and a complete system of ribbed vaults which must certainly be due to French inspiration. This is borne out by much of the surviving decorative detail both here and at the abbey. The only surviving Cistercian churches are those of Kercz, founded in 1202, and Apátfalva, founded in 1232. Both are of the normal Cistercian type except that Kercz has a polygonal apse in place of the square east end. Kercz also has a system of ribbed vaults, whereas the later church at Apátfalva has groined vaults in the German tradition.

A strong German influence was introduced into Hungary by Gertrude, the German queen of Andrew II, whose open and unashamed favouring of her countrymen led to her assassination in 1213. It is with this German influence that the last group of definitely Romanesque churches of Hungary is connected. They include the Benedictine abbeys of Lébény (1206–10), Jaák (1210–41), Türje (c. 1240), and Zsámbék (before 1255), and a number of minor and derived churches. They follow a uniform plan of an aisled basilica with apsidal chancel, sometimes projecting side apses, and a pair of western towers opening into the nave and aisles by open arches. In general the type is south German as is the general scheme of architectural decoration, but there is no reflection of the German fondness for the double bay and the arches opening into the towers are again not a German feature. The twin west towers, on the other hand, may well have been inspired by the Austrian cathedrals of Brixen (Trentino), Gurk, and Sekkau, and the towers themselves are typical of the German-Lombard style with arcaded bands between the stories, and the same bands are continued along the eaves and round the apses. The roofs have been much altered, but it appears that the ribbed vault had been generally adopted. The round arch is still in general use for the smaller openings, and even in the main arcades of Lébény and some of the doorways are the richest examples of Hungarian Romanesque decoration. The west doorway at Jaák has an elaborate series of enriched orders and jamb-shafts, which include, curiously enough, the chevron, embattled, and lozenge ornaments. Even at this date, however, there are remains of the Italian tradition, for the outer shafts of the doorway are based on the backs of carved lions, a feature which was also present in the destroyed porch of the cathedral of Esztergom (Gran) and dating from c. 1200–9. The cathedral of Gyulfehérvár (Alba Julia) in Transylvania, hardly finished before the Tartar invasion of 1241–2, is still largely Romanesque both in plan and in its apsidal chapels. Here, however, a return is made to the transeptal form. The rebuilding towards the end of the century was undertaken by a Frenchman, and the visit of Villard

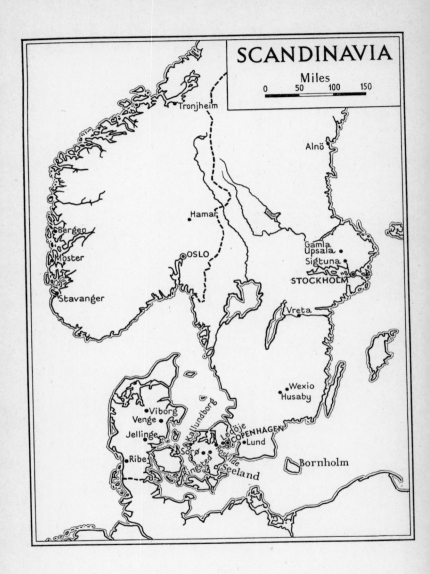

SCANDINAVIA

Miles

0   50   100   150

Tronjheim

Alnö

Bergen

Moster

Hamar

Stavanger

OSLO

Gamla
Upsala
Sigtuna

STOCKHOLM

Vreta

Wexio
Husaby

Viborg
Venge

Kallundborg

Jellinge

Ledöje

COPENHAGEN

Lund

Ribe

Sorø

Ringsted

Roskilde

Seeland

Bornholm

de Honnecourt in 1244–51 is thought by many to have directly influenced the abandonment of the Romanesque style and the readoption of French Gothic forms.

SCANDINAVIA

The Romanesque architecture of Scandinavia must necessarily be confined to the period or type in which the material is stone or brick. These structures were preceded by a highly remarkable class of building in timber, which includes the celebrated mast or stave-churches of Norway and cognate buildings in the other Scandinavian countries. In structure these buildings are purely native, and their elaborate decoration provides the latest and most florid examples of what may be termed Viking art, into which Romanesque motives only occasionally intrude themselves.

In general, Scandinavian Romanesque is a mixed art to which Germany and England both contributed, the German elements preponderating in Denmark and the English in Norway and parts of Sweden.

Denmark. Though an organized church was established in Denmark in the middle of the tenth century, it has left no tangible traces of its existence. Its buildings were no doubt of timber, and it is not till a century later that stone churches seem to have come into use. The early connexion was entirely with Hamburg and Germany, and it was not until the establishment of the empire of Knut the Great that any English influence is to be expected.

The earliest group of stone churches in Denmark, known as the Roskilde group, belongs to the second half of the eleventh century and was mainly due to Vilhelm, Bishop of Roskilde (1060–74), and Svend Nordmand (1074–88), his successor. Remains have been discovered of the cathedral of this period, and of the abbey church of Ringsted, while considerable portions of V.F. church at Roskilde still survive. The cathedral was a simple aisled church with an aisleless chancel and a square west end projecting between two towers. V.F. church, Roskilde, was a simple aisled church with apses at the ends of the aisles and an apsidal chancel. It has square piers and round arches, a simple clerestory, and much of the masonry is set herring-bone wise. It seems probable that this simple basilican type was introduced from the south, though the use of herring-bone work was perhaps learnt from England. A building of definitely English inspiration is to be found in the well-preserved Benedictine church of Venge.[1] Here the small transepts with their comparatively narrow entrances are in the Anglo-Saxon tradition, while the square chancel with its apse are of Anglo-Norman type. With the building of the three chief surviving Romanesque cathedrals of Lund (now in Sweden), Ribe, and Viborg, the influence of Germany becomes definitely paramount. At Lund, which will be dealt with later, the model was perhaps Speyer; at Ribe (begun c. 1130) the material used is Rhenish tufa and the design of the three-storied interior indicates a copying from S. Ursula, Cologne, or some similar church. Viborg, the latest of the three, is a granite church following the general lines of Lund.

To the age of Waldemar I the Great (1157–82) and Archbishop Absolon (d. 1201) belongs the next group of churches, which include the earliest brick buildings of Denmark. The most important and best preserved examples are in Seeland— Ringsted Abbey, Sorø Abbey, Kallundborg, and Vitskøl Abbey, the last, a Cistercian church of highly unusual plan, founded by Waldemar after the 'Blood Banquet' at Roskilde (1157).

A notable feature of Danish Romanesque is the prevalence of the round church of which there are numerous examples in Bornholm. The German type of double-chapel is represented at Ledöje in Seeland, while the remarkable late twelfth-century church at Kallundborg, ascribed to Esbern Snare, is a centrally planned church with five towers, one in

---

[1] F. Beckett, in *Aarbøger f. Nordisk Oldkyndighed*, 1918, p. 35.

the middle, and four, of octagonal form, over the four projecting chapels or transepts.

In decoration, Danish Romanesque, while borrowing much
from Germany and little from England, retains here and
there traces of its earlier native art. Thus the 'great-beast'
of the Jellinge rune-stones still makes an occasional appearance, and the remarkable carved pediment of the south doorway at Ribe is as distant from German as it is from English
sculpture. Here and there, too, use is made of the Italian lion
as a support for a shaft or column.

In some ways the most remarkable survival of Romanesque
art is in the gilded metal altar-frontals of which some seven
still exist in the country.[1]

Sweden. The first attempt to convert the Swedes accompanied by the founding of a church at Birka in the ninth
century has left no remains, and it was not until the eleventh
century that the attempt was repeated. This time the impulse
came from England, through Norway, and early in the century
St. Sigfrid[2] and his companions established themselves at
Husaby, Wexio, and elsewhere; it is thus that the earliest
surviving stone churches show considerable traces of English
influence. At Sigtuna on Lake Mälar are the ruins of two important churches (Figs. 57–8)—S. Peter and S. Olaf—and
perhaps traces of a third which belong to the age when Sigtuna
was the most important ecclesiastical centre of Sweden. S.
Peter's Church is a cruciform building with the two axial
towers of Anglo-Saxon tradition, windows with mid-wall
shafts, and other features of the same origin. The three apses,
however, show Norman influence, which accords well with
the date assigned to it by H. Cornell,[3] *c.* 1080–1100. S. Olaf's
Church (*c.* 1100–34) is a more advanced structure with aisles
to the chancel and nave, and a central tower supported, or

---

[1] P. Nørlund, *Gyldne Altre*, 1926. There are also two in Sweden and
one in Norway.   [2] *Acta Sanctorum*, Feb., ii. 848 et seq.
[3] H. Cornell, *Sigtuna och Gamla Uppsala*, 1920.

formerly supported, on twin arches. The plain battered lines of this tower are still in the Anglo-Saxon tradition, and the twin arches may be compared to those of the west tower of the 'minster' at South Elmham, Suffolk. Similar supports to the tower are to be seen in the church at Gamla Upsala[1] (1134–c. 1150), which is still partly in use and stands on the site of a square timber structure which may well have been the great Pagan temple described by Adam of Bremen[2] which it supplanted.

Gamla Upsala was a simple cruciform church with an aisled nave, central tower, transepts, and chancel, each with an apse. This form is repeated at Vreta Abbey (first half of the twelfth century) and may have been inspired by S. Knut's (1080–6) Church at Lund if we accept Rydbeck's theories of the arrangement of this building. The existing cathedral (Fig. 56) at Lund, which may incorporate parts of its predecessor, was begun c. 1123, when the crypt was under construction. Its architect, Donatus, was presumably an Italian both from his name and from features of the architecture and decoration, which are Lombard in character; the arcaded gallery round the main apse seems to be earlier in date than any established example in Germany. The simple arcades of the earlier building were transformed into the double-bay system, one bay of the main building equating with two in the aisles. The west towers are probably an addition to the original design, and the west doorway has a projecting outer order standing on columns which is definitely Italian in origin.

Romanesque decoration in Sweden, except for certain features at Lund, is not remarkable for richness. Certain churches in west Gothland[3] are markedly English in character

---

[1] The see was removed from Sigtuna to Gamla Upsala c. 1135.

[2] Adam of Bremen, *Gesta Hamma, Ecc. Pont.* iv, chap. 26.

[3] See articles by E. Fischer in *Västergötlands Fornminnes.* Tidskrift (1918), 9–10.

and display a certain amount of crude figure-carving closely allied to early twelfth-century work in England. The decoration also includes a free use of interlacement, chevron-ornament, and a foliage of Ringerike or late Viking type. Sweden has preserved an unusual number of early fonts, some of them elaborately decorated. Among these may be mentioned the very remarkable example carved in pinewood at Alnö.

Norway. The conversion of Norway, begun under Olav Trygvasøn (995–1000), was forcefully completed by Olav the Saint (1016–30). As far back as the half-Christian king Haakon the Good (d. 961) all its ecclesiastical associations were with England, and both Olaf Trygvasøn and S. Olav obtained their first bishops and priests from that country.

Stone building was hardly introduced into Norway before about 1100, and thus the little church at Moster, long identified with that built by Olav Trygvasøn, must really belong to a much later date. The larger Romanesque churches of the twelfth century seem to be derived from two sources, those of the south and east showing the influence of Denmark and Germany, while those of the west owe more to the Anglo-Norman school. The earliest example of the south-eastern type would appear to have been Halvard's cathedral at Oslo, which was partly finished by 1130 when Sigurd the Crusader was buried in it. It was a three-aisled building with a central tower, transept, and apsidal choir. The ruined cathedral of Hamar, dating from the foundation of the see in 1152, is perhaps the latest example of the type, and had two western towers which, as we have seen, were an addition to the cathedral of Lund. Both these churches had cylindrical piers to the nave, and chapels flanking the choir. The type would seem to have been directly influenced by the German churches of the Hirsau school, both in the general plan and in the use of cylindrical piers. The western type was perhaps first exemplified at Christchurch, Bergen, but the evidence of its original arrangement is by no means complete. The best preserved example is Svitun's cathedral at Stavanger which closely resembles a large Anglo-Norman aisled church without transept and with a western tower. To the same influence belongs the much more elaborate structure of S. Magnus' cathedral, Kirkwall, Orkney, begun in 1137, and not completed till the thirteenth century. This church with a transept and central tower shows evidence of the influence of Dunfermline and Durham in the treatment of the original cylindrical piers, and the square chapels east of the transept were perhaps copied later at Tronjheim.

S. Mary's church, Bergen, is the earliest church displaying a triforium, and here also we find the use of compound piers. It possesses in addition perhaps the most elaborate Romanesque doorway in the country. It is now generally agreed that the Romanesque portions of the cathedral of Tronjheim (Nidaros) were begun about 1152, when the see was raised to metropolitan status. To this period belongs the transept which was added to the west of the earlier church erected by Olav Kyrre (1066–93) over the tomb of S. Olav. The aisled nave, of which foundations have been discovered, was never completed. The chapel in the south transept was consecrated in 1161. The early church of Olav Kyrre was replaced by the existing choir in the thirteenth century.

The decoration of the Norwegian churches appears to owe most to the Anglo-Norman school. The chevron-ornament appears frequently throughout the country, and the cable and billet ornament make a more occasional appearance. An interesting carved marble head inscribed 'Eystein rex', found near the monastery founded by that king in Bergen *c.* 1100, perhaps belongs to the middle of the twelfth century.

SUMMARY BIBLIOGRAPHY

ARCHITECTURE.

G. Dehio and G. von Bezold, *Die kirchliche Baukunst des Abendlandes*, 1884–1901.

P. Frankl, *Die frühmittelalterliche und romanische Baukunst*, 1926.

F. Ostendort, *Die deutsche Baukunst im Mittelalter*, i, 1922.

M. Aubert, *Congrès archéologique de France, Rhénanie*, 1922.

G. Dehio, *Geschichte der deutschen Kunst*, 4th ed., 1930.

H. Christ, *Romanische Kirchen in Schwaben und Niederfranken*, i, 1925.

J. Hecht, *Der romanische Kirchenbau des Bodenseegebietes*, 1928.

A. Zeller, *Die romanischen Baudenkmäler von Hildesheim*, 1907.

—— *Die frühromanischen Kirchenbauten und Klosteranlagen nördlich des Harzes*, 1928.

F. Beckett, *Danmarks Kunst*, 1924, 1926.

H. Fett, *Norges Kirker i Middelalderen*, 1909.

—— *Nordisk Kultur-Kunst*, 1931.

L. Gál, *L'Architecture religieuse en Hongrie du XIᵉ au XIIIᵉ siècles*, 1929.

SCULPTURE.

G. Dehio and G. von Bezold, *Die Denkmäler der deutschen Bildhauerkunst*, 1905.

H. Karlinger, *Die romanische Steinplastik in Altbayern u. Salzburg 1050–1260*, 1924.

F. Novotny, *Romanische Bauplastik in Österreich*, 1930.

R. Ligtenberg, *Die romanische Steinplastik in den nördlichen Niederlanden*, 1918.

H. Beenken, *Romanische Skulptur in Deutschland*, 1924.

E. Panofsky, *Die deutsche Plastik des elften bis dreizehnten Jahrhunderts*, 1924.

INDEX

208INDEX

Westminster Abbey, 141, 143.
Wexio, 191.
Wilfrid, St., 8.
William I, of Sicily, 50, 55.
William II, of Sicily, 50, 53, 55, 56 *n.*
William of Hirsau, Abt., 162.
William of Volpiano, St., 27, 91, 138, 145.
Wimpfen im Tal, 172.
Winchester Cathedral, 140, 141, 142, 143, 147, font, 184.
Windberg, 162.
Wing, 19.
Worcester Cathedral, 141, 147.

Worms: Cathedral, 161, 164, 165, 166, 184; Synagogue, 177.
Wulfric, Abt. of Canterbury, 28, 145.
Würzburg: Cathedral, 164, 168; Festamarienburg, 8, 172.

York: Minster, 147; Virgin, 152, 181; St. Mary's Abbey, 141.

Zadar (Zara): Cathedral, 71, 72; Chapel, 172 *n.*; S. Crisogono, 71; Sta. Maria, 72.
Zamora, 125; Cathedral, 120, 121.
Zsámbék, 188.

1. Cividale,
Tempietto

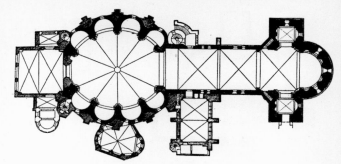

2. Cologne, S. Géréon

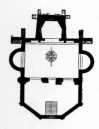

3. Poitiers, Bap-
tistery of S. Jean

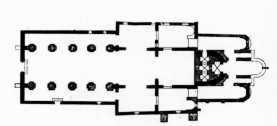

4. S. Philbert de Grandlieu

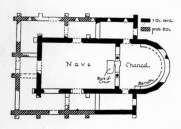

5. Reculver

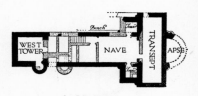

6. N. Elmham

(48 feet = 1 inch)

0   25   50   75   100 feet

(*Figs.* 1, 5.)

(72 feet = 1 inch)

0   25   50   75   100 feet

(*Figs.* 2, 3, 4, 6.)

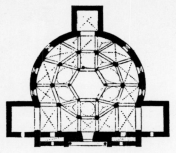

7. Benevento, Sta. Sofia

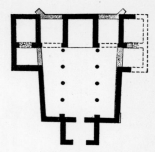

8. S. Juan de Baños

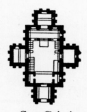

9. Sta. Cristina
de Lena

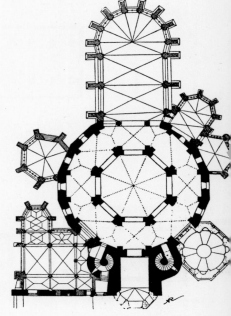

11. Germigny-
des-Prés

10. Aachen Minster

(48 feet = 1 inch)

(72 feet = 1 inch)

(*Figs.* 8, 9, 11.)

(*Figs.* 7, 10.)

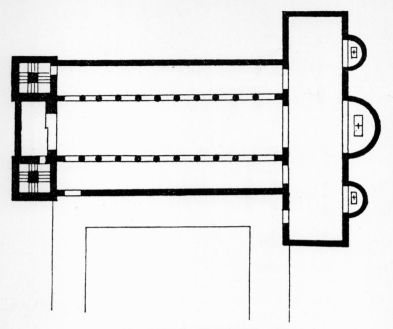

12. Hersfeld. Carolingian Church

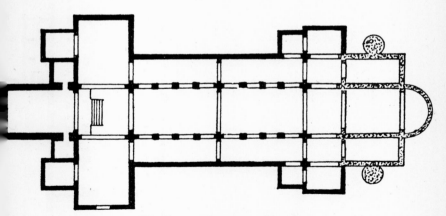

13. Nivelles. 11th-century Church

(72 feet = 1 inch)

0   25   50   75   100 feet

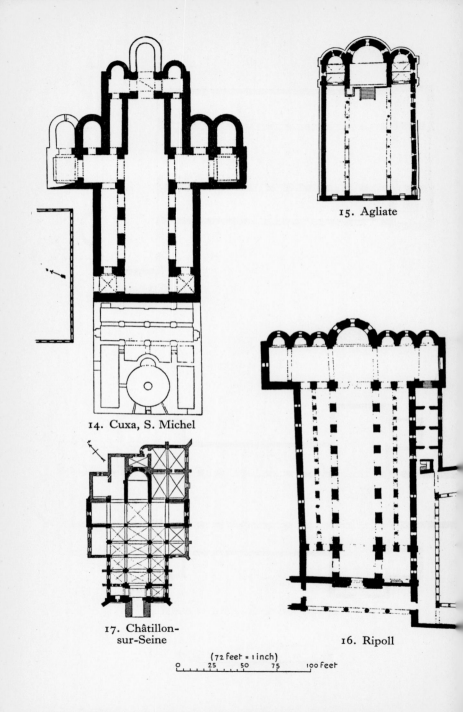

14. Cuxa, S. Michel

15. Agliate

17. Châtillon-
sur-Seine

16. Ripoll

(72 feet = 1 inch)
0   25   50   75   100 feet

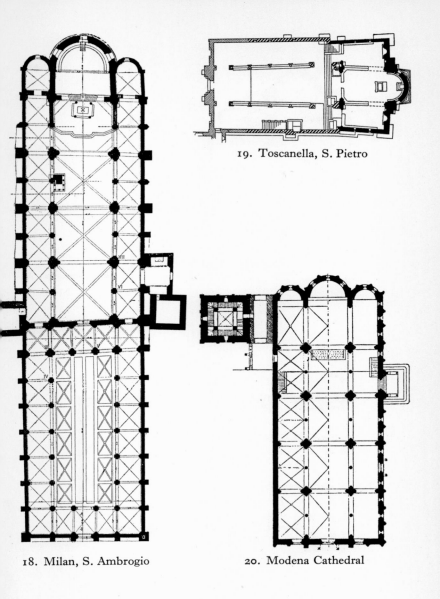

19. Toscanella, S. Pietro

18. Milan, S. Ambrogio

20. Modena Cathedral

(72 feet = 1 inch)

0   25   50   75   100 feet

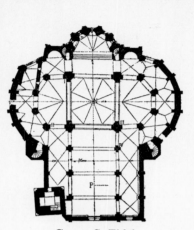

21. Como, S. Fidele

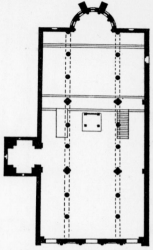

22. Florence, S. Miniato
al Monte

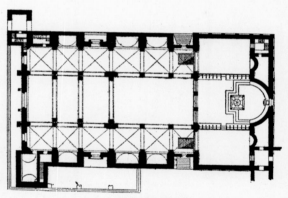

23. Bari, S. Nicola

(72 feet = 1 inch)

0   25   50   75   100 feet

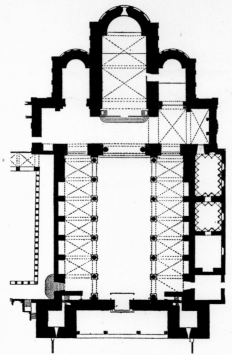

24. Cefalù Cathedral

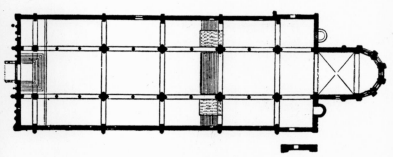

25. S. Zeno, Verona

(72 feet = 1 inch)
0   25   50   75   100 feet

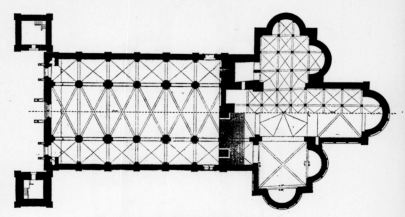

26. Parma Cathedral

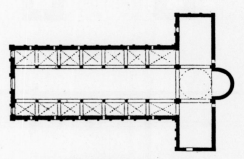

27. Pisa, S. Paolo a ripa d'Arno

(72 feet = 1 inch)

0   25   50   75   100 feet

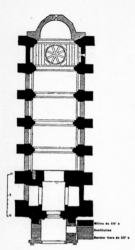

28. Avignon Cathedral

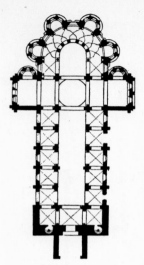

29. Clermont, N.-D.
du Pont

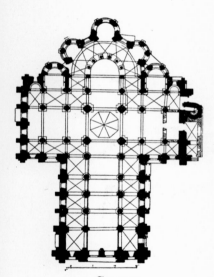

30. Conques

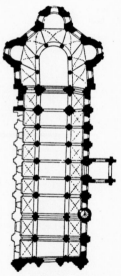

31. Poitiers, N.-D.
la Grande

(72 feet = 1 inch)
0   25   50   75   100 feet

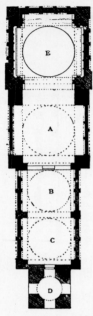

32. Périgueux, Old
Cathedral

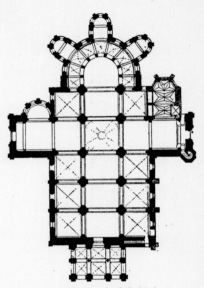

33. Paray-le-Monial

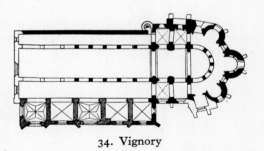

34. Vignory

(72 feet = 1 inch)
0   25   50   75   100 feet

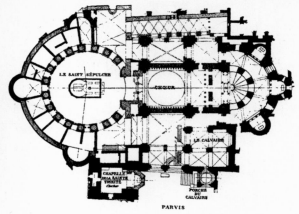

35. Jerusalem, Holy Sepulchre

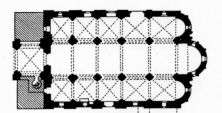

36. Beyrout Cathedral

(72 feet = 1 inch)
0   25   50   75   100 feet

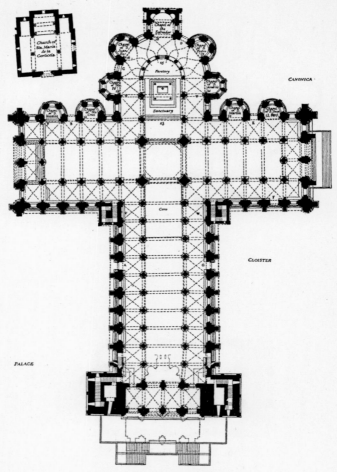

37. Compostela Cathedral

(72 feet = 1 inch)
0   25   50   75   100 feet

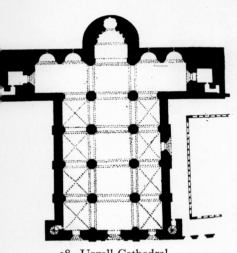

38. Urgell Cathedral

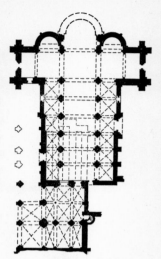

39. León, S. Isidoro

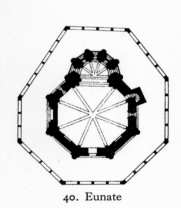

40. Eunate

41. Toro

(48 feet = 1 inch)

0   25   50   75   100 feet

(*Fig.* 40.)

(72 feet = 1 inch)

0   25   50   75   100 feet

(*Figs.* 38, 39, 41.)

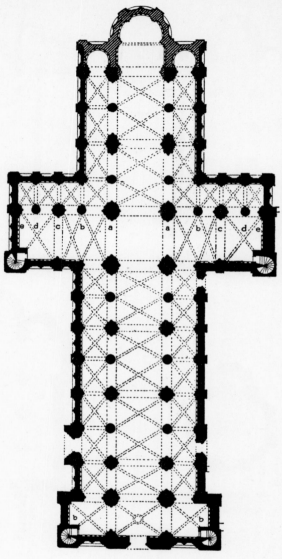

42. Durham Cathedral

(72 feet = 1 inch)

0   25   50   75   100 feet

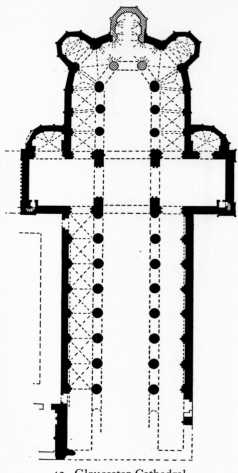

43. Gloucester Cathedral

(72 feet = 1 inch)

0   25   50   75   100 Feet

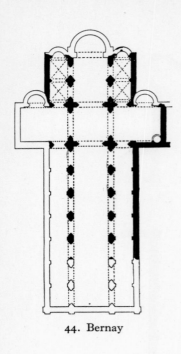

44. Bernay

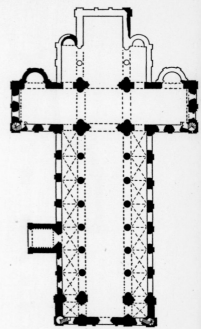

45. Southwell

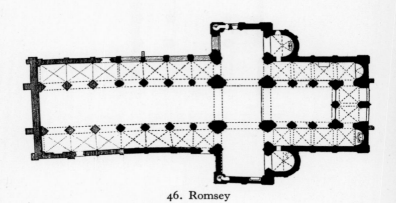

46. Romsey

(72 feet = 1 inch)

0   25   50   75   100 feet

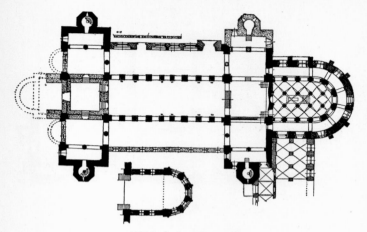

47. Hildesheim, S. Michael

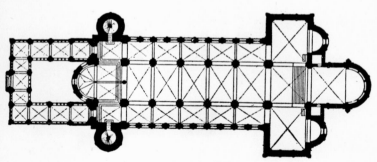

48. Maria Laach

(72 feet = 1 inch)
0   25   50   75   100 feet

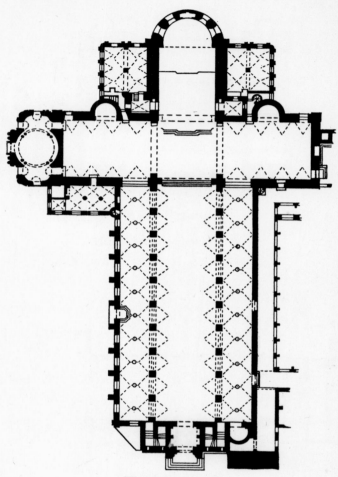

49. Würzburg Cathedral

(72 feet = 1 inch)

0   25   50   75   100 feet

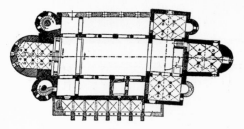

50. Gernrode

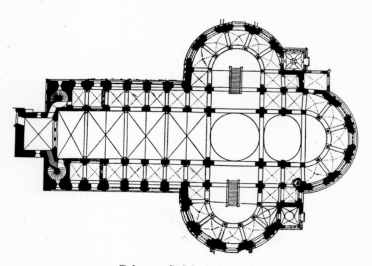

51. Cologne, S. Maria im Kapitol

(72 feet = 1 inch)

0   25   50   75   100 feet

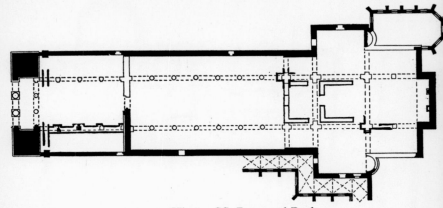

52. Hirsau, SS. Peter and Paul

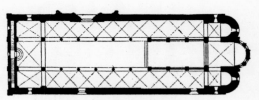

53. Regensburg, S. Jakob

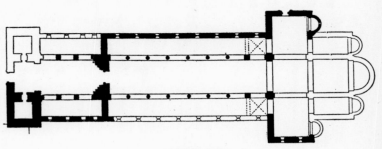

54. Paulinzelle

(72 feet = 1 inch)
0   25   50   75   100 feet

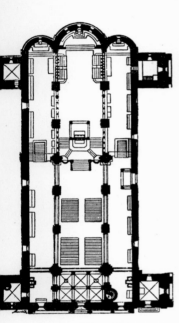

55. Pécs

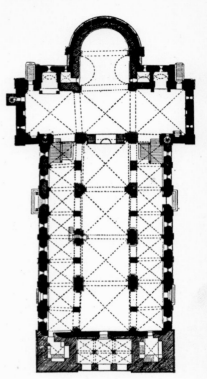

56. Lund

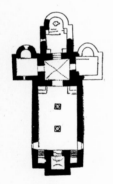

57. Sigtuna,
St. Peter

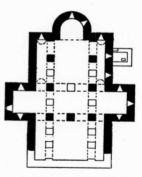

58. Sigtuna, St. Olaf

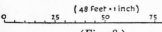

(48 feet = 1 inch)

0   25   50   75   100 feet

(*Fig.* 58.)

(72 feet = 1 inch)

0   25   50   75   100 feet

(*Figs.* 55–7.)

PLATE I

ITALY

b. CIVIDALE. Tempietto, 8th–9th cent. (?)

a. CIVIDALE. Pemmo Altar, 744–9

PLATE 2

a. LISBON CATHEDRAL. Carved ornament, 7th cent.

b. POITIERS. Hypogeum. Carved ornament, 7th cent.

PLATE 3

a. S. MARIA DE NARANCO. SPAIN. Interior, *c*. 848

b. BRIXWORTH (Northants.) Interior, late 7th cent.

PLATE 4

a. LEÓN. Stele,
4th–5th cent.

b. EASBY. Cross-shaft,
late 7th cent.

PLATE 5

a. LORSCH. GERMANY. Torhalle, 8th–9th cent.

Photograph by Staatliche Bildstelle, Berlin

b. POITIERS. FRANCE. S. Jean, 9th cent. and earlier

PLATE 6

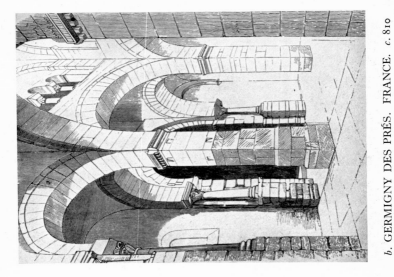

b. GERMIGNY DES PRÊS. FRANCE. c. 810

a. AACHEN. GERMANY. Minster, 796–804

Photograph by Staatliche Bildstelle, Berlin

PLATE 7

a. AGLIATE. ITALY. E. end of church, *c*. 875

b. TUSCANIA (Toscanella). ITALY. E. end of S. Pietro
Late 11th cent.

PLATE 8

a. CHATILLON-SUR-SEINE. FRANCE
E. end of church, *c*. 991

b. CUXA. FRANCE. S. Michel, *c*. 974 and *c*. 1020

PLATE 9

a. TOURNUS. FRANCE. Narthex. S. side, *c*. 1000

b. TOURNUS. FRANCE. Narthex. Interior, *c*. 1000

PLATE 10

a. RIPOLL. CATALONIA. Church from S.E. *c*. 1032, restored

Photograph by Arxiv Mas

b. CARDONA. CATALONIA. Church from S.E. *c*. 1020–40

Photograph by Arxiv Mas

PLATE II

ITALY

b. FLORENCE. S. Miniato al Monte, 11th cent.

a. PAVIA. S. Michele. Early 12th cent.

PLATE 12

ITALY

a. MILAN. S. Ambrogio. Nave. Early 12th cent.

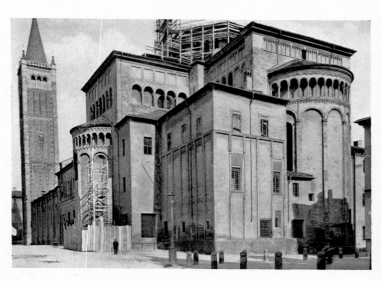

b. PARMA CATHEDRAL from the S.E. 12th cent.

PLATE 13

ITALY

b. TROJA CATHEDRAL. c. 1093–1127

a. LUCCA. S. Michele. 12th cent.

PLATE 14

ITALY

a. BARI. S. Nicola. *c.* 1089–1135

b. BITONTO CATHEDRAL. Begun 1175

a. CEFALU CATHEDRAL. Begun 1131

b. MONREALE CATHEDRAL. 1174–82

PLATE 16

ITALY

b. RUVO CATHEDRAL. W. doorway
13th cent.

a. PAVIA. S. Pietro in Ciel d'oro
Consecrated 1132

PLATE 17

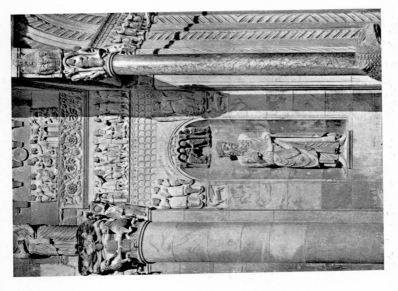

b. FIDENZA (Borgo S. Donnino) CATHEDRAL
W. front. End of 12th cent.

a. VERONA. S. Zeno. W. doorway
c. 1135

ITALY

a. PISA. Baptistery. Begun 1153

b. BARI. S. Nicola. Throne. 1098

PLATE 19

FRANCE

a. CARPENTRAS CATHEDRAL. Frieze. Mid to late 12th cent.

b. S. GILLES DU GARD. W. front. Mid 12th cent.

PLATE 20

FRANCE

b. CLERMONT. N. D. du Port. Early 12th cent.

a. TOULOUSE. S. Sernin. Consecrated 1096

PLATE 21

FRANCE

POITIERS. N. D. la Grande. Mid 12th cent.

PLATE 22

FRANCE

VÉZELAY ABBEY. Nave. Early 12th cent.

PLATE 23

FRANCE

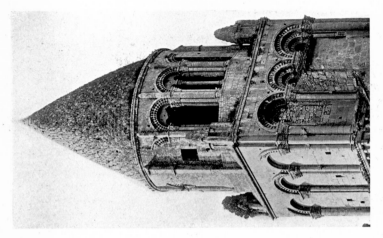

b. SAINTES. S. Marie des Dames
Tower. Mid 12th cent.

a. SOUILLAC. c. 1130–40

PLATE 24

FRANCE

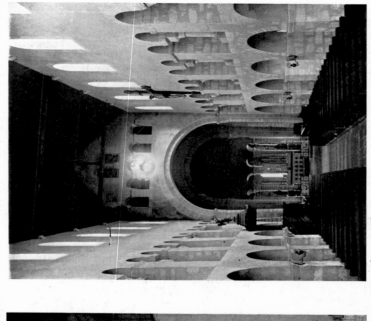

b. VIGNORY. Nave. c. 1050

a. CLUNY. S. transept. c. 1110

PLATE 25

FRANCE

c. SOUILLAC
c. 1130-40

b. TOULOUSE. S. Étienne
c. 1130-40

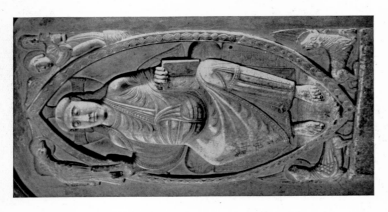

a. TOULOUSE. S. Sernin
c. 1096

PLATE 26

FRANCE

a. MOISSAC. Tympanum. *c.* 1120

b. VÉZELAY. Tympanum. *c.* 1120

PLATE 27

FRANCE

a. AUTUN. Eve in the Garden. 12th cent.

b and *c*. CLUNY. Capitals from apse. *c*. 1095

PLATE 28

HOLY LAND

a. JERUSALEM. Holy Sepulchre. Mid 12th cent.

b. NAZARETH. Capital. *c*. 1187

PLATE 29

SPAIN

LEÓN. S. Isidoro. *c.* 1100 and mid 12th cent.

PLATE 30

SPAIN

b. SAHAGÚN. S. Lorenzo
12th cent.

a. SALAMANCA. Old Cathedral
Consecrated 1160

PLATE 31

SPAIN

SILOS. Cloister. Panel and capitals. Early 12th cent.

PLATE 32

SPAIN

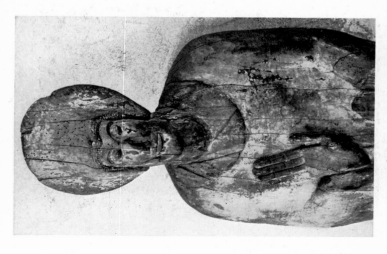

a. TAHULL. Virgin. *c.* 1123

b. RIPOLL. W. façade. 1150–75

PLATE 33

FRANCE

b. BERNAY ABBEY. c. 1017–50

a. JUMIÈGES ABBEY. c. 1040–67

PLATE 34

ENGLAND

b. BLYTH PRIORY. Nave
Late 11th cent.

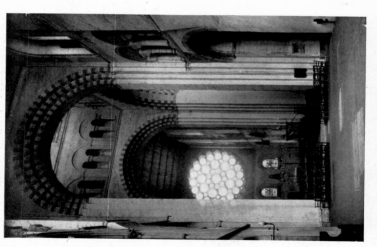

a. ST. ALBANS ABBEY. Crossing
Late 11th cent.

PLATE 35

PLATE 36

ENGLAND

a. BARNACK. Christ
Early 11th cent. (?)

b. YORK CATHEDRAL. Virgin
and Child. *c*. 1000 (?)

a. ELY CATHEDRAL. S. doorway. *c*. 1150

Photograph by Starr and Rignall, Ely

b. FOWNHOPE. Tympanum. *c*. 1150

PLATE 38

GERMANY

a. WORMS CATHEDRAL. 11th, 12th, and 13th cent.
Photograph by Staatliche Bildstelle, Berlin

b. MARIA LAACH ABBEY. Early 12th cent.

PLATE 39

b. KORVEY. W. front. 9th and 12th cent.

Photograph by Staatliche Bildstelle, Berlin

a. FRECKENHORST. Consecrated 1129

Photograph by Staatliche Bildstelle, Berlin

PLATE 40

GERMANY

a. PAULINZELLE ABBEY. Nave. Early 12th cent.

b. SCHWÄBISCH GMÜND. Nave. Late 12th or early 13th cent.

PLATE 41

b. MAINZ CATHEDRAL. Nave aisle
Early 12th cent.

a. HILDESHEIM. S. Michael. Early 11th and
late 12th cent.

PLATE 42

GERMANY

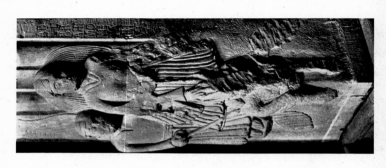

a. GERNRODE ABBEY. The Marys at
the Sepulchre. Mid 12th cent.

b. WORMS. Flight into Egypt
Mid 12th cent.

PLATE 43

PADERBORN. Externstein. Descent from the Cross. Early 12th cent.

PLATE 44

GERMANY

REGENSBURG. S. Jakob. Schottenthor

c. 1200